PHOENIX FIRST ASSEMBLY
13613 N. Cave Creek Rd.
Phoenix, AZ 85022

THE SOUL PATROL

"Here Comes the God Squad"

by BOB BARTLETT

With Jorunn Oftedal

LOGOS INTERNATIONAL

PLAINFIELD, NEW JERSEY

—

Library Oakland S.U.M.

Fountain Trust
Central Hall
Durnsford Road,
London, SW 19, England

© copyright 1970 by
Logos International
Plainfield, New Jersey
All rights reserved
Printed in the United States of America

This book or parts thereof may not be reproduced
in any form without permission of the publisher.

Library of Congress number 71-107609
SBN 912106-02-6

Second Printing September 1970

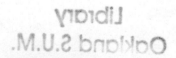
Library
Oakland S.U.M.

To my wife Ona, our children,
the friends and co-workers in
Teen Challenge, especially
The God Squad, this book is
dedicated.

PREFACE

The fight is on.

There's a battle going on between right and wrong, between light and dark, between the real and the counterfeit.

It's a battle where no one can be neutral; we're born into it; we've got no choice.

There is no such thing as a cop out. There's nowhere to go.

You can't stop the world and get off. You're on it, you're part of it.

Sometime in our life we all have to choose between the real and the counterfeit, the right and the wrong.

Are you confused about what's what? Does the wrong look right and the right look wrong?

Jesus said: You know a tree by its fruits.

You know the right and the wrong by its consequences. Jesus also said that if you ask you will get answers; seek and you'll find; knock and the door will be opened.

This book is about some kids who made a choice; they

found the real. Some of them were drug addicts; others were hung up on sex or money or popularity or false security.

I believe that we are all born with an instinctive knowledge of what is right and wrong, real and phony.

At one point in our lives we see the choice, we feel that tugging inside.

The kids in this story came to that point; they got honest with themselves and with God and said "yes" to His tugging inside them. They answered the call.

Some of them came from the gutters, some from the back pews of suburban churches. God called them together, He made them into a team. He sent them into battle.

I

"WE ARE THE GOD SQUAD,
Mighty, mighty God Squad
Everywhere we go . . .
People want to know . . .
Who we are . . .
So we tell them:
WE ARE THE GOD SQUAD!"

I LOOKED at the clock on my desk. 10 p.m. That sounded like Kathy and Karen singing in the hallway, and they weren't due back till near midnight. Could anything be wrong?

All of us at Teen Challenge run on a tight schedule. We usually operate in areas of the city where anything can happen, and if some of us don't report in on time someone else goes out to look for us.

This evening Karen and Kathy had been assigned to the team that was working out of Hidden Manna, our coffeehouse near Rittenhouse Square, Philadelphia's hippie hangout. The Square is far from being the safest spot in the city. There is often heavy drug traffic, and homosexuals and lesbians are looking for pickups. Our team walks the park in twos, inviting anyone to visit our coffeehouse, where we offer "free coffee and discussion on religion."

Sometimes the kids in the park give our fellows and girls a hard time. That's how we got our name in the first place; someone started yelling after two of our girls: "Here comes the God Squad . . . look out for the God Squad . . ."

I could hear Karen and Kathy starting up the stairs toward the girls' dorm. Surely they had seen the light in my office window. Why didn't they check in? I got up and went to the door.

This is the part of my job as director of Teen Challenge that I find most difficult, knowing that in a sense I am responsible for each one of our staff members. Of course I know that each one came because he felt God calling him. God has a job for each one and His protection surrounds them. But still, there is crime and violence on the streets where we go, and there have been some close calls . . .

I went out into the hallway and called up the stairs.

"Hi, girls! What are you doing back—" The last words stuck in my throat. Karen and Kathy turned and smiled at me broadly. They looked like half-drowned kittens, clothes dripping wet and hair plastered down with what seemed to be gobs of saliva. Kathy had a long scratch on the side of her face, and Karen's jacket had a ripped sleeve.

"What happened?" I stammered. "Are you hurt?" They both shook their heads vigorously.

"It was nothing, just a bunch of kids in the Square getting carried away."

I finally got the whole story.

The evening was warm and the kids in the Square were restless.

"They were standing in groups or sitting and lying on the grass," Karen said. "Somebody was playing a guitar, and you could hear the beat of a bongo drum. It's hard to describe, but you could feel the restlessness—almost like electricity in the air, just waiting for a spark."

The girls had walked almost through the park without incident when suddenly somebody yelled at them from the dark shadows under a tree.

"Come here, baby, tell me all about Jesus." They recognized the broad mocking grin, the inevitable white T-shirt over flexing muscles, the black Afro-bush and the beads. Jimmy has been a pain in the neck for months. He is a regular at the Square and all of us from Teen Challenge have had our experiences with him. He follows our teams around, mimics them, teases, and dances around like a clown. Of course he has a big following of admirers, and when he is high on drugs, which is most of the time, there is no telling what he'll think of next. Jimmy is no dummy. He's read more than most, and one of his favorite pastimes is to come down to the coffeehouse and give some of us a rousing argument about religion. Lately he has become more bothersome than usual, and naturally he is a constant subject for prayer among our workers. I have heard my wife Ona sigh from her heart, "Dear God, please don't let Jimmy bother us tonight. Keep him away. Do something, Lord!"

One thing was apparent—God wasn't keeping him away. Jimmy was always there.

Tonight Jimmy's remark had all the impact he must have hoped for. Almost instantly Karen and Kathy found themselves surrounded by a jeering, laughing, and jostling crowd.

"Yeah, come tell us about Jesus. Why don't you ask Him to come here? We'd like to meet Him—" The girls had been in tight spots before and stood silently praying while the kids around them got noisier by the second.

Suddenly a blob of saliva hit Karen in the back of the head. The crowd roared excited approval, and the two girls became the targets for a rain of spit, curse words, and obscenities. They felt themselves jostled around, then lifted high on strong arms, carried over the heads of the cheering mob, and dumped with a splash into the shallow water of the fountain.

Jimmy stood like a black giant, arms folded across his chest, feet set wide apart, watching the two soaking wet girls climb out of the fountain. His face wore a sly, triumphant smile. The crowd behind him was silent, waiting for a sign.

"You don't need to tell me about Jesus," Jimmy proclaimed, chuckling to himself. "I am Jesus, I know all about Him." The crowd looked from Jimmy to Karen and Kathy, then back again. This was the kind of cat and mouse game they loved.

"I could hear Karen praying softly next to me," Kathy said, "and the fear that had settled like a tight little ball in my stomach just dissolved, and suddenly I felt warm and good—as if I was in the safest spot in the world. I looked up at Jimmy and opened my mouth; I didn't even know what I was going to say, except I knew it was going to be all right."

" 'You do know all about Jesus, Jimmy, I know you do—' There was a flicker of something in Jimmy's eyes. They were glued on mine. 'And Jimmy, Jesus knows all about you—'

"It got so quiet around that all you could hear was the sound of water trickling from the fountain. You could tell something was going on inside Jimmy. Then all of a sudden he tossed his head and turned to the kids in the crowd. 'Let's go,' he said, and strode quickly down the path under the trees. Without looking back the whole crowd followed him silently."

Karen and Kathy had breathed a quick, "Thank you, Jesus," and run the two blocks to the coffeehouse.

"We're just going to change our clothes and go back—if you'll let us, Brother Bartlett," Karen said, fingering her ripped sleeve. I shook my head in disbelief.

"Why don't you just take it easy and get some rest," I suggested. "You've been working late every night this week." Both girls looked at me with long faces.

"Please!" Kathy's brown eyes were suddenly moist. "I thank God Jimmy is getting worse," she said. "You know it means Jesus is getting to him—I know. I used to be that way." She grinned that impish grin of hers, and I couldn't help laughing. Sure, she knew. She'd come to Teen Challenge two years ago, a college sophomore, boy-crazy and pregnant. How well I remembered her attention-getting temper tantrums.

I nodded at the two girls and watched as they ran up the stairs singing vigorously: "We are the God Squad . . . mighty, mighty God Squad . . ."

I leaned my head against the back of my chair and glanced at the stack of papers waiting on the desk. On top was the note in Sunday's firm handwriting: "Don't worry about the thousand dollars—the prayer chain is going!" I wanted to groan out loud. Always bills stacked high, and now a thousand dollars due on a gasoline bill in two days. Thank God for Sunday. She's been with us almost from the start, giving up a lucrative job with an oil firm to come here and work long hours with a hopelessly unpredictable budget and no salary at all. But Sunday never thinks of our operation as unpredictable.

"You know God isn't going to let that bill get overdue," she often reminds me. "He's never left us dangling yet."

No, He hasn't. But it is sometimes hard to remain calm and confident when we are operating on a budget of nearly $100,000 a year and our bank account seems permanently stuck somewhere below $50.00.

Now in the summertime our regular staff of 40 is augmented by student volunteers from Bible colleges across the country. We serve at least 200 meals a day on a $100 a week budget, and sometimes our cooks perform miracles from practically bare cupboards.

This last year we've opened three branch-centers in the greater Philadelphia area, and here at the Main Center we're bursting at the seams. Our girls sleep three bunks high in an overcrowded dorm and we've got to get a girls' house soon. Besides, the center at 1620 North Broad Street is in an area where it is getting increasingly dangerous to walk the streets, even in daylight. We're just at the edge of the black ghetto.

I closed my eyes and I could almost hear Ona's calm voice in my ear.

"Look, honey, don't fret. God knows every one of our needs. This is *His* center and He certainly doesn't need for you to worry about it."

The phone rang at my elbow and I jumped. The voice at the other end was that of an older man, sober, but obviously upset.

"Mr. Bartlett? . . . Please, may I bring my son to you? He's a dope addict." I interrupted before he could continue.

"Does your son want to come?" From the silence at the other end I knew the answer. "I want to help," I said, as gently as I could. "But we can't do anything for your son unless he really wants help." The man was blowing his nose. It sounded like a muffled trumpet blast in my ear, and I wanted more than anything to tell him, "Come on, bring your son, I'll promise a miracle." We've seen plenty of miracles around here—but they never happen against the will of an addict.

"Please, my son is sick," the man was pleading with me. "Won't you just talk to him?"

Just then the door to my office opened and Danny put his head in, winked at me, then pulled Judi after him. They stood in front of my desk, holding hands, beaming from ear to ear.

"Please, Mr. Bartlett—" In that instant I remembered another father, another desperate, "Please talk to my son!"

I sat bolt upright in my chair.

"Okay," I said into the receiver. "Bring your son in as soon as he gets off his high. I can't promise anything, but I'll talk to him." I hung up before I could change my mind, and caught the glance Danny was exchanging with Judi.

"Thanks, Bob," Danny said. "If it hadn't been for *my* dad, who knows where I'd be today . . ." His voice trailed, then his face brightened again. "Boy, we had a great trip to Wisconsin." He launched into an excited description of their two weeks' tour through the Midwest, where he had spoken to high school assemblies and preached in churches of several denominations.

"Kids all over are looking for reality," he said eagerly, sitting on the edge of his chair. "They rebel against everything phony both inside and outside the church. They aren't running from reality when they try the drug scene; they're just looking for something real." Danny nodded toward the street outside. "Boy, do we have competition out there! The people who push this rebellion sure have some beautiful sounding words: peace—free love—instant religion—freedom from all this phony, sordid confusion. Get all this in a nickel bag, a needle, or a pill. By the time they figure out it's counterfeit, they're hooked."

Danny was off on one of our favorite subjects. If kids could only have half a chance to hear the real story about the power of God and Jesus Christ and the Holy Spirit—if they could only get a taste of the real freedom and peace and love . . .

Unfortunately traditional Christianity has left a lot of kids —and adults too—with a bad taste in their mouths. Watered down, formalized religion, not telling it like it is. Not showing any evidence of what can happen in the lives of those who really discover the truth.

Of course, that's why we are here, working practically around the clock at Teen Challenge, Philadelphia. Not just to help drug addicts and homosexuals and alcoholics and unwed mothers, but to tell it like it is to every young person, wherever God will send us.

You don't have to be a drug addict to need the power of God in your life. I discovered that when I was a teen-ager in Arkansas City, Kansas. I was captain of the church basketball team and didn't think I could come up against anything I couldn't handle. I was used to getting things my way. What upset me was a girl who wouldn't give me a date. I don't remember her name anymore. She was just a slip of a girl, and I really thought she'd jump at the chance of going to a dance with me, the big shot. (Humility wasn't one of my strong points.) She wouldn't go to the dance and even said "no" when I suggested we take in a movie. By this time she'd made me pretty upset, and I was determined to keep at it till I got my way. At last she agreed to go out with me—if I'd take her to church!

It so happened that she belonged to a church where the power of God was very evident. I had never seen anything like it. I noticed a whole group of kids there from my school. They were the guys who didn't cheat on exams and the girls who wouldn't park on a dark lane.

Never had I heard such singing and such praying! For once in my life I was faced with something I didn't understand at all. I went with those kids to somebody's house for cokes and popcorn, and before the evening was over I knew that my new friends had fun in a way I'd never tried before—the kind where you don't have a bad taste in your mouth the next day; you don't have to stretch the truth when you tell your mother about it; and the light was never turned off.

The next evening I was invited to come along to a revival in a small country church. It was really a converted school house. I can't explain why I went, something just drew me. I sat on a hard wooden bench and felt something churn around in my stomach and burn inside my chest. My knees felt numb and I had only one straight thought in my head: *I need what those kids have and I've got to get it!*

Before the service was over I stumbled up to the home-made altar and there I knelt, the fifteen-year-old cocky captain of the basketball team, crying my heart out. I didn't know how to pray, but a little old lady came up and knelt next to me and started praying with me. All I knew was that I had been all wrong in the way I'd tried to run my life till then, and I kept saying over and over again, "God, I'm sorry. Jesus, please help me." And suddenly something happened inside me that I can't explain. But I can't explain electricity either, I can just describe it. I know it turns on the light. And that night a light was turned on inside me, and I knew that from then on God was running my life.

Seven years later I sat in a prison in New York and looked across the table at a skinny teen-ager with sullen brown eyes. His father had committed him to the court to keep him from killing himself with drugs. Our time was short and I didn't mess around with a lot of words.

"Danny," I said, "there's a power more real than any drug you've ever been high on. It can change your life; it can change you. It is light and peace and love and truth and it works. It works for me. Jesus Christ can do it for you, and He needs you."

That's how I met Danny, and that's how God recruited the first member of His God Squad for Teen Challenge, Philadelphia.

II

IF I'D had it my way we would never have ended up in Teen Challenge. Ona and I were both going to Bible College in Waxahachie, Texas. She was majoring in elementary education and we were in perfect agreement about our future. In a little over two years I would graduate, and we would seek a pastorate in some middle-sized town somewhere in the Midwest. We weren't too specific about where, except we knew that we absolutely did not want to go to a big city on the east coast.

We were both quite outspoken on this point for several reasons. We'd never been to the East, but what we had read only strengthened our aversion. Both of us had grown up in the Midwest—Ona on the outskirts of Tulsa, Oklahoma—and we didn't want to settle too far from our families. Besides, we wanted security and hoped to raise children in peaceful surroundings.

Ona had another, more personal reason, though she didn't talk about it much. She had always been shy and preferred being alone with a good book rather than being in a crowd. Me, I was the complete opposite. I loved to be with people and could talk freely about personal problems and deep convictions. For the last several months I'd been aware that Ona was fighting her own personal battle. She was sixteen when we got married, and now, two years later, I knew that she was going through an emotional crisis. She was always careful not to complain. I was usually the one who came home and unburdened my soul, Ona the one who listened patiently.

But lately it had been obvious that something was threatening to overcome her. When I asked, she'd smile bravely and say, "Don't worry, God's taking care of it."

I was getting concerned, however. Several times I had come home from class in the middle of the day to find the door to our trailer home bolted securely from the inside and the blinds drawn. I had to pound on the door and shout before Ona would peek carefully out from behind the curtain, then open the door to let me in. She was baby-sitting in the afternoons for a friend, and she had little Scotty beside her on the couch, quiet as a mouse. It looked like they'd both been sitting there, reading.

Sometimes in the middle of the night I would wake up suddenly, as Ona was frantically grasping my arm, her frightened eyes searching the room around us.

"What's wrong, honey?" I'd listen for a strange sound that might have startled her, but heard nothing. Our trailer was parked securely on the campus of the Bible College. Nothing or no one could possibly harm us.

"Bob, I'm afraid. Pray with me." We would pray, and the horrible fear I had seen in her eyes would go away. But soon it would come back.

I knew that Ona had gone to our pastor's wife and asked her to pray also. Whenever I asked Ona what she was afraid of, she could only shake her head and say she didn't know.

"Honestly, Bob, I don't understand. It comes over me—sometimes at night, sometimes in the daytime—and I'm just sure that someone or something is going to get me."

Ona had grown up in a moderately well-to-do home with loving, Christian parents. All her life she had been loved and cared for, had never lacked anything, had never felt threatened. Yet here was a fear so overwhelming that it was about to paralyze her.

I put my arms around her and inwardly cried out to God: "Lord, she's my wife and I want to protect her from the fear of whatever it is. Help us, God." I'd never felt so inadequate in my life.

One morning, before classes, I went into the chapel and knelt alone in the front pew. "God," I prayed out loud, "You've got to help me. I want to give my wife the security she needs, but I don't know how." I stayed there on my knees for quite a while but nothing happened. I didn't get any bright and dazzling revelation. The peace I was praying for didn't come to soothe the restlessness and confusion I felt. I walked out of there feeling wretched. Surely there was an answer. Either God was silent or I was too thick-skulled to hear Him. This whole thing was getting me down more than I was willing to admit, even to myself.

A book lay on the hall table in the classroom building that day. Absentmindedly I picked it up: David Wilkerson: *The Cross and the Switchblade*. The thought flashed through my mind, *Boy, it's a good thing we're not gonna preach the gospel to killer-*

*happy drug addicts in a ghetto. Ona sure would have something to be
scared of then!*

Almost without thinking I put the book in my pocket.
David Wilkerson and Nicky Cruz would be coming to our
campus soon to speak, and I thought I'd like to read about
them first.

Ona wasn't at home when I got to our trailer. The door
was unlocked, so she couldn't be far away. Her Bible was on
the table and she had circled a verse in red: "There is no fear
in love, but perfect love casteth out fear." (1 John 4:18)

Slowly I sat down. The letters in the verse seemed to be
dancing before my eyes. What a fool I had been! I should have
known better all along. I'd felt helpless and inadequate and
had asked God to help *me* protect my wife. *Me* protect her. As
if that could ever be enough. When would I ever learn my lesson?

"I'm sorry, God," I prayed. "Maybe one of these days
You'll get it through my thick skull that our only protection is
in You. Forgive me for not trusting You, God. Forgive me for
thinking I had to do the job for You. Just please take care of
my wife."

I looked up. Ona was standing in the doorway, a grocery
bag in her arms, a big smile on her face.

"Hi, honey." She glanced toward the open Bible. "It's
really great! I've been saying that verse over and over to myself all the way to the store and back, and as long as I keep
saying it and thinking it I'm not the least bit afraid."

Over the next several weeks Ona's battle against fear continued, but with a difference. Sometimes, at night, I woke to
find her sitting up in bed speaking in a quiet but determined

voice into the darkness: "There is no fear in love, perfect love casteth out fear. God is love, I am in Him. You've got no hold over me, fear." Over and over she'd say it until all tenseness was gone from her voice. Then with a soft, "Thank You, Jesus," she would lie down and go back to sleep almost instantly.

The bouts with fear were coming less often and were getting easier to overcome each time. We talked about it once or twice, wondering why the whole thing had happened in the first place. Ona couldn't find any obvious explanation. One thing was certain. She had always been easily frightened by strange situations; now she was able to go places and do things she never thought she could do before.

As springtime wore on, we began to take a group of 100 or more students to Dallas on weekends, going out on the street in pairs, handing out tracts, and witnessing to young people. Never before had Ona been able to do anything like that without feeling all bound up inside, her stomach in a knot of fear. After a couple of weekends in Dallas she told me triumphantly that the technique of quoting 1 John 4:18 to herself worked beautifully on the street.

"It's a matter of spiritual willpower, you know," she explained earnestly. "Our will and God's power. He's given us the tool to overcome anything. All we have to do is stick to it."

One day there was a knock at the door of our trailer. Outside stood a young couple we knew briefly in school.

"Hi, there," the young man greeted us. "We thought perhaps you'd like to sell your trailer—" Ona and I looked at each other, then up and down our street where several trailers had large "For sale" signs.

"You've made some kind of mistake," I told him. "We have another two years to go in school. Why would we want to sell our trailer?" The couple looked at us, then at each other with obvious perplexity.

"Sorry to have bothered you," the young man said. "But we really thought you wanted to sell."

After they had left, Ona looked thoughtful. "What in the world do you think gave them that crazy idea?"

"I don't know," I said lightly, but there was a familiar feeling inside, as if something was about to happen. I was sure Ona felt something too. Her eyes followed me around searchingly.

"Bob," she asked, "are you up to something?"

"Honestly, honey," I said, "I'm as puzzled as you are. If we're not supposed to be here in school for the next two years I sure haven't found out about it yet."

I needed to spend a couple of hours in the library. Before leaving, I handed Ona the David Wilkerson book. It had made a deep impression on me. Maybe it would take her mind off the puzzle about the trailer. It was Tuesday night and David Wilkerson and Nicky Cruz were due in Dallas for a weekend rally on Friday.

Wednesday morning I got up early and started across campus to a 7 a.m. class in theology. It was a sunny morning in May and the campus looked bright and beautiful. I felt good and breathed in the crisp morning air thinking that just then I wouldn't want to be anyone else, anywhere else, in the whole wide world.

Suddenly, from somewhere behind me, came a blood-curdling scream. I froze on the path and looked carefully all around. I could see nothing. The sun shone over the wide lawns and neat shrubbery. There wasn't a living soul in sight.

I thought perhaps I wasn't quite awake yet; I must have been dreaming. I shook my head, turned, and continued walking toward the library where our class was meeting, and I heard the scream again. It was a terrible scream, and suddenly I felt as if a Presence was with me. I stood all alone in the middle of the path and felt as if I had suddenly shrunk to nothing, and all around me was the Spirit of God. I don't know how I knew, I just knew, and clear as a bell the words came to my mind: "Son, the scream you just heard is a scared and lonesome drug addict on the street of a large eastern city. He'll die, and unless you go he won't ever know My love and My way."

All I could do was whisper, "I'll go, just show me, I'll go." I went on to class in a half-daze and spent the rest of the day trying to sort out my jumbled thoughts. Every so often I'd tell myself, "Bob, you've gone stark raving mad!" but I knew that was a poor way to squirm out of a tight spot. I'd heard enough testimonies from reliable, sane people who had seen and heard some very specific messages from God that I couldn't convince myself that the whole thing was a figment of my imagination. I knew better. Deep down I knew God had called me to do something for Him, and I had better obey. But how? Two more years till graduation; I had a job after school; we were making payments on the trailer, a brand-new washing machine, and a new air-conditioner. And what about Ona? When I handed her the David Wilkerson book, she had glanced at the cover, then laughed.

"Whatever you do, Bob, don't ask *me* to go someplace like that!"

During the next two days I spent a considerable number of hours on my knees. Slowly my state of confusion gave way to a

feeling of certainty. God was the One who had done the calling; obviously He had planned the whole thing. All I could do
was wait for Him to show me the next step.

Ona seemed preoccupied and I was grateful. I caught her
looking at me once or twice as if she wanted to ask me something, but she never did. At that point I don't think I could
have given her a sensible answer about anything.

Friday night at the Wilkerson rally I served as an usher,
and during the altar call I looked up to see David Wilkerson
looking straight at me. As soon as he caught my eye he motioned for me to come up on the stage. I went up and he came
right to the point.

"Have you thought of coming to Teen Challenge?" I stood
motionless and thought, *Surely that man is looking straight through
me.* "Some preachers in Philadelphia are interested in seeing a
Teen Challenge Center started there," he went on. "You could
come to New York and work with me first." When he mentioned Philadelphia, something registered inside me, something said, *This is it!*

"I'd like to talk some more about it," I told him. Dave
Wilkerson nodded and asked, "Are you married?"

"Yes," I answered, and he said he would like to talk to my
wife. I found Ona in the crowd and brought her to the stage.
She'd always been an expert at hiding her feelings; it was impossible to tell from the look on her face whether she approved
of the idea or not as David outlined briefly for her what he had
in mind, and then he said to both of us: "God will call each of
you separately. That is always a sign. I'll be on the campus tomorrow, give me your decision then." I glanced at Ona. She
was smiling at David Wilkerson, but she didn't say a word.

On the way home she was quiet. I asked her how she felt

about the situation and she wouldn't answer. It wasn't like her. We'd always discussed the pros and cons before making any major decisions. I'm the impulsive one, ready to take off and get carried away, and she's the calm, level-headed one who gets my feet back on the ground. In our entire married life I'd never suggested anything quite as radical as the proposal David Wilkerson had just thrown at us, and here she sat, refusing to say anything at all one way or the other. I fumed in wordless distress.

We went to bed in utter silence, and there, in the dark, I felt Ona's hand slipping into mine.

"Honey," she whispered softly, "don't pay any attention to me. You've got to trust God and listen to what He is saying to you. Then make your decision."

Ona slept soundly all night while I tossed and turned. Saturday I worked in the plastics factory till four o'clock, and by the time I got home I was literally sick. Ona had supper ready, but I couldn't get a bite down. She looked at me across the table, and I tried to read her thoughts.

"What are you going to tell Mr. Wilkerson?" she asked. I shook my head.

"I don't know," I said. "I just don't know." I went to bed and tried to pray: "God, You know I want to do Your will, but what if Ona doesn't want to go?" I got no answer, just the sound of Ona washing dishes and humming to herself. How could she?—at a time like this? I groaned and turned over on my stomach.

I thought of Ona and all the things I'd wanted to give her in the future. How proud she'd been when I got her the washing machine for Valentine's day! She *loved* that silly machine. I'd wanted to give my wife the best of everything—she certainly deserved it. How could I ask her to go live in a stinking ghetto?—Ona, who still quoted 1 John 4:18 to keep from being afraid of the dark. What was it she'd said to me last night? "Trust God?"

"Lord, show me what to do!" I prayed.

Suddenly Ona was standing in the doorway. "If you don't get ready, we'll be late for the meeting," she said. There was a light over her face and I thought I'd never loved her more. And all at once I knew what God wanted me to do.

"What are you going to tell David Wilkerson?" Ona's voice was calm. I stood up and looked in her eyes.

"I'm going to tell him we'll come," I said. Without a word Ona turned and left the room. I wanted to run after her, take her in my arms, and tell her I'd do whatever she wanted us to do, but something held me back. What was it Jesus had said? ". . . unless you are ready to leave your mother and your father and your wife . . . and follow me!" God had called me. I had to answer, and I had to trust God to take care of the rest.

"Go with her, Jesus," I prayed.

During the meeting I had only one thought—I had to get to David Wilkerson and give him my decision before I could change my mind. He met me halfway down the aisle and his face brightened when I told him what I had decided.

"Great!" he said, shaking my hand vigorously. "We'll be expecting you as soon as you graduate in June."

"Graduate?" The word almost stuck in my throat. "I won't graduate for another two years." David Wilkerson looked as if somebody had hit him with a wet rag. Then he shook his head and looked slightly apologetic.

"Sorry, Bob, I misunderstood. I can't use you until you

graduate. Drop me a line in a couple of years if you're still interested."

I felt numb. Without a word I turned and went out. I motioned for Ona to follow me, and I didn't say a word till we were back home in the trailer. Then I spilled the whole story, in angry, tumbled words. She listened quietly, and when I was talked out she touched my arm and said gently, "Who called you to Teen Challenge, Bob? David Wilkerson or God?" Time stood still and the presence of something far greater than both of us seemed to fill our trailer and push the walls beyond where we could see. Ona's hands were clasped in mine, and there were tears in her eyes. Something wet was rolling down my own cheeks, and I pulled Ona close.

"You know," I whispered into the soft fragrance of her hair. "God called."

Ona pulled away; her eyes held mine firmly. "When God has called us," she said, "He doesn't leave us dangling." She pulled me over to the kitchen table. "Sit down," she said. "I've got something to tell you."

Tuesday night she had read David Wilkerson's book in one sitting, so caught up in the story that she couldn't put the book down. Wednesday she had come home after classes and started cleaning the trailer when suddenly she began to cry uncontrollably, aware that she was crying over the lonely and desperate drug addicts in the ghettos of our big cities. (I had heard the scream on my way to class Wednesday morning.)

"I thought maybe I was just being emotional," she said. "I'd just read *The Cross and the Switchblade* and I knew that David Wilkerson was coming to our campus soon. So I prayed, but I just kept crying, feeling the burden for those poor kids heavier and heavier. Finally I got on my knees and told God that if He was making me feel this way because He wanted us to go East to work, He'd have to make you decide without me. In fact, I made it real hard and said you'd have to make the decision thinking that I didn't really want to go."

When David Wilkerson had said that God would call each of us separately, she almost said something, but held back, knowing that my decision had to be based on God's call, and not be swayed by her opinion.

"So now let's go back and talk to Wilkerson," she said briskly, tugging at my hand. "I'm sure God will show him, too."

Monday, David Wilkerson was interviewing students for summer jobs. He was in the dean's office, and I walked in and asked if we could talk to him again. He sat slumped over behind the dean's desk and he looked tired.

"Sorry, Bob," he said. "I just can't use you now—"

"But my wife has something to tell you," I interrupted. I saw a glimmer of interest in David's eyes. Ona stepped up to the desk and as soon as she began talking he sat bolt upright in the chair, listening intently as Ona recounted our experience to him.

"So you see," Ona concluded, "we really don't have any choice. God has called us to come now, and we can't very well refuse the call."

David leaned forward eagerly, his eyes alive with excitement. "I believe God called you too!" Then he explained: "You need to get a "Home Missions" appointment in order to get permission to raise money for your support through your church. *Ordinarily* you have to graduate in order to get such an appointment. But in your case—" he paused briefly as if to make sure his guidance was true. "Yes, in your case, go ahead and try. We'll just trust God to work everything out. If you can raise your own support and settle everything by September, come along to New York. I'll put you to work."

Monday we were both home for lunch when someone knocked at our door. Outside was the same couple who had come by a week ago. The young man looked a bit sheepish, but blurted out, "We're sorry to bother you again, but are you *sure* you don't want to sell your trailer?" I started laughing and had to double up to keep my sides from hurting. Ona invited them in.

"It's quite a coincidence," she said. "As a matter of fact, God has just decided we *do* want to sell it."

III

WITH all the odds stacked against us we went to Springfield, Missouri, to seek appointment as home missionaries for the Assemblies of God churches. Appointments were rarely given to anyone who hadn't graduated from college. I had been associated with the Assemblies for less than two years, Teen Challenge was a relatively new mission field, and we were very young. I was barely twenty-one and Ona was only eighteen.

We knew that the Home Mission Board met twice a year at Springfield, but we didn't know when. Arriving with our application, we were told that the Board was in session that very day. They agreed to see us, listened to our story, and within two hours we had our appointment!

Till then we hadn't allowed ourselves to get really excited. But that day, driving home toward Tulsa in our beat-up old car, we laughed and sang and thanked God for His influence on Home Mission Boards. We also thanked Him in advance for the way He was going to raise money for our support, pay off our school bills, and get us a new car.

Over the next three months He took care of it all—including Ona's washing machine. She didn't want to sell it.

"Please, Bob—we'll need it in New York. Can't we get a trailer and haul it with us?"

"Let's pray about it," I suggested, and she shook her head.

"If we pray, I know what'll happen—I'll have to sell," she complained jokingly.

We prayed during my lunch break from school. When I came from class that afternoon I asked her if she had sold the washing machine.

"Did you have to ask right away?" she protested, looking a little embarrassed. "Just after you left Judy came to see me. She said, 'Ona, I came to buy your washing machine.' She had the money with her—so what could I do?"

We marvelled together at how God was directing our path.

A few days later we went to Tulsa, Oklahoma, Ona's hometown, and asked a bank for a loan to buy a new car. The bank manager looked at us and scratched his head.

"You mean you're going all the way to New York? You're going to work on practically no salary, preaching to drug addicts, and you want a loan?"

I nodded and he scratched his head again and looked surprised.

"You know I have to send somebody to get your car if you can't make the payments—" I nodded again. "Well, it doesn't make any business sense at all," he said, looking perplexed. "But I'll do it."

And so the practical problems concerning our move were all taken care of. We kept getting the feeling that God was always one step ahead of us. But it wasn't quite so easy to handle the human side of it. Ona's parents weren't at all happy about letting their teen-age daughter—even though she was married—walk the streets of New York City working with drug addicts. Our friends and my teachers in school all seemed to be firmly against the idea. One of my professors even offered to pay my last two years' tuition if I'd consider finishing college before leaving.

"If this is God's idea, why are all these people so much against it?" I asked Ona one day. I was getting tired of defending myself.

"So who are you trying to please?" she asked me. "God or people?"

I knew the only answer to that—but still I wished I could please everybody. I realized that I had better get used to living with opposition. All my life I'd been outspoken, but I had also been quite aware of people's opinion of me. I didn't like it when I felt that someone disapproved. It was hard to stand up against the challenging questions of men whose opinions I had learned to value and respect. They seemed to have my best interests at heart—

Yet, if I was really serious about letting God direct my life, I would have to learn to accept the criticism and disapproval of others. I couldn't be swayed by the arguments of men. I would have to learn to trust God completely.

Early in September of 1963 we packed the new car full of our belongings. Ona and I squeezed together under the steering wheel and headed for New York City. Our great adventure was under way.

All we really knew about Teen Challenge and New York was from David Wilkerson's book, Nicky Cruz's testimony, and rallies we had attended. We were convinced that what awaited us would be exciting and thrilling. There might be even a little touch of danger to make our crusade for God into the sophisticated jungles of the East more daring.

I couldn't wait to see David Wilkerson again.

"What do you think he'll say when he sees us?" I asked Ona. "I bet he'll want to put me to work right away."

Looking from the New Jersey side, New York City was bigger and more confusing than I'd expected. But I soon found it's a lot easier to look at something big from the outside than to be stuck right in the middle not knowing where to go. We arrived at the portals of the Holland Tunnel during the peak of the rush hour. I was caught in the maelstrom being sucked down into the tunnel going to Manhattan, and just as we were spewed out into the daylight again, our car stopped dead, right in the middle of an intersection. Bedlam broke loose around us—horns hooted and brakes squealed and we just sat there.

"God," I prayed out loud, "I know You didn't get us here to desert us in the middle of this mess. Get us out, please!" My prayer was short but as fervent as I could make it.

Just as I thought the end had come, in the form of a huge diesel truck looming at us from one side and a policeman descending from the other, our car started up again. Ona looked like she was getting homesick for Oklahoma already.

"Don't worry, honey," I said. "Just think how great it will be to meet everybody at Teen Challenge. Remember, God sent us."

She managed a pale smile.

416 Clinton Ave., Brooklyn. We'd read about it till we thought we knew all about it. Now, at last, we were here. We

— 27 —

PHOENIX FIRST ASSEMBLY
13613 N. Cave Creek Rd.
Phoenix, AZ 85022

parked our car on the street, locked it securely, and climbed the steps to the front door. We rang the bell. Once, twice . . . finally someone came to the door, looked at us and the dust-covered car with Oklahoma plates, and asked: "Who are you, and what do you want?" We stepped in hesitantly.

"Reverend Wilkerson told us to come," I replied. "The Lord has called us to work at Teen Challenge." I tried to sound confident and enthusiastic, but at this point I was discouraged, exhausted, and badly in need of a bath.

"Wilkerson is out of town. He didn't say anything about you—" The young woman looked at us skeptically—and I couldn't blame her. I wanted to turn and march out that door. I felt crushed.

The girl turned her head and yelled over her shoulder to someone in another room: "Two kids are here—they say Brother Wilkerson told them to come to work. Do we have any place to put 'em?" She sounded as if she was expecting a negative reply.

Was this our grand entrance to New York? I felt two inches high, and when I looked at Ona she was staring straight ahead, biting her lip. I could tell she was fighting back the tears.

Just then an attractive woman came out into the hall. When she saw us she smiled warmly. "Don't worry, kids," she said. "Everything will be all right." I wanted to hug her. That smile of hers was the most beautiful thing I'd seen since we left home.

They put us in a small room on the third floor, known as the girls' floor. We sat on the edge of the bed, staring at each other and at our pile of luggage in the middle of the room. I felt the whole thing was a mess—but I tried to keep telling myself that God had sent us there.

Utterly woebegone, I looked at Ona. She started to force a smile, but suddenly her eyes were sparkling and we were having fits of laughter. We laughed till we cried.

"You know, Bob, we really needed this." She was laughing so hard she could barely talk. "We were feeling like big shots, like God was really lucky to have us come to Teen Challenge. We needed to be brought down a couple of notches." We had been brought down all right.

I don't know why I always see my mistakes afterward, instead of ahead of time. I make a fool of myself and wonder why I get my feelings hurt. There are always plenty of warnings too—if I'd only heed them. I've never made a mistake yet that I haven't found a warning about later—in the Bible.

That evening, on our knees in the little room on the third floor at Clinton Avenue, we looked again at the verse I've had to underline in Romans 12:3: "For I say . . . to every man that is among you, not to think of himself more highly than he ought to think; but to think soberly, according as God hath dealt to every man the measure of faith." I had to underline a verse in Paul's first letter to the Corinthians, too: ". . . let him that thinketh he standeth take heed lest he fall." (I Corinthians 10:12)

On our knees we prayed, "Okay, God, we see our mistake. It's Your show again, Lord, and please keep us from grabbing any of the credit. Teach us from scratch what You want us to learn here in New York. Even if You've got to make us scrub floors and peel potatoes. Use us to *Your* glory and for *Your* purposes. And God, keep us humble."

We didn't peel potatoes or scrub floors, but we did learn a

lot of things from scratch. Both of us felt that God had called us to go to Philadelphia one day, but we also realized that first He had to get us ready for the job.

Ours wasn't the kind of work you could learn from a textbook, even if there had been such a book. Some things we learned by working side by side with people who had dealt with drug addicts for years. We learned how to recognize symptoms of the prolonged use of alcohol or drugs, and we saw some of the ways of coping with the problems. We learned from the success stories and perhaps even more from the failures. With God's help we learned through experience.

Before coming to Teen Challenge I'd never seen the stark reality of human beings in desperate need. I'd never seen people so stuck in the quicksand of addiction to alcohol or drugs or sex that they were too helpless even to ask for help.

What bothered me the most were the ones who could still carry on fairly normal lives outwardly. They were still fooling most of the world—their parents, their teachers, their bosses, their husbands or wives, and the police. Worst of all, they were fooling themselves. And no one could help them until they acknowledged their need for help.

"I'm not an addict," they'd say. "I can quit this stuff any time I want to, but why should I? It's great! I won't get hooked." Behind their boasting show of confidence we could see they were "hooked" already.

I'll never forget my first visit to a "shooting gallery"—a place where addicts go to "shoot up" on dope.

I was assigned to work with English-speaking addicts. There weren't many who spoke English at the center since we were located in a largely Spanish-speaking neighborhood, and so I went out on my own to comb the streets for junkies. Nicky

Cruz was working on the streets with Spanish-speaking addicts. I knew that Nicky's dedication and zeal paid off as a number of addicts were set free from their habit.

Night after night I walked, often till two o'clock in the morning. Gradually I became acquainted with the addicts and their hangouts. They, in turn, got used to seeing me around. They knew who I was and what I was doing and they knew I wasn't "the man" as they called the law, or a "nark," as they called the narcotics agents. I wasn't trying to "bust" them or turn them over to the police.

One night I stopped outside a candy store where many of the junkies in the neighborhood came to buy their "stuff." A fellow I had talked to several times was just leaving the store with two of his friends. He smiled when he saw me and said, "Hi, Bob."

"Hi!" I said. "I'll buy you fellows a cup of coffee." Of course I knew they had just bought some dope and were probably on their way to shoot up, but I had nothing to lose, I thought, and I might at least detain them for a while.

Billy shook his head. "It's no use, Bob," he said. "We like what we're doing—that's the way it's gonna be and you know it."

He stood directly in front of me. Without taking my eyes from his I reached out and put my hand on his arm.

"Billy, tell me what you see in that stuff," I said. "Why does it have such a hold on you?"

Billy returned my gaze steadily. "Why don't you come along and find out for yourself," he challenged.

I looked at Billy's two friends as they exchanged questioning glances and then nodded in agreement.

"Okay," I said. "Let's go."

We walked around the corner and stopped in front of a narrow brownstone apartment house which looked like it ought to be condemned. None of the other houses on the block looked much better. Billy glanced quickly up and down the street, then led us up the stairs from the sidewalk and into the nearly dark hallway. The stench of urine and sour garbage just about drove me out again. I had to breathe through my mouth to keep from getting nauseated. Billy kicked a couple of empty cans aside and started up the creaking stairway.

Although the house was dilapidated, it was certainly not deserted. Noises of every description came from behind the thin doors and walls as we groped our way up several flights of stairs in the darkness—babies crying, adults yelling, radios blasting rock and roll, and the din of television turned on high to drown out the neighbor's set.

We reached the fifth landing and the fellows stopped. In the blackness I could hear one of the boys moving around. It sounded as if he was lifting a loose board. Then there was the flash of a match, and I saw Billy kneeling on the stairway before an opening in the wall. He reached in and found the stub of a candle, which he lit and placed on the stairs. I had guessed right; he had removed a loose board and now brought out everything they needed for a "fix"—a hypodermic needle, an eyedropper, a grimy-looking ketchup bottle filled with water. The three fellows huddled close together, two of them watching intently as Billy took a small package from his pocket. He opened it carefully, exposing the innocent-looking white powder. One of the other fellows took the lid off the ketchup bottle and held it, while Billy poured the powder into the lid, taking care not to spill a single grain. Then he added a few drops of water from the bottle and held the mixture over the candle.

The three seemed hypnotized. I don't think they would have noticed if the roof had fallen in. I saw the strange gleam in their eyes, their faces taut and tense, and I felt a sudden chill, as if I was in the presence of an invisible evil power. The whole scene had a nightmarish quality, and I thought, *This is crazy. There must be a way to break the spell. I've got to stop these fellows!* I leaned forward and Billy looked up, his eyes flashing a warning as he hissed the words from behind clenched teeth: "Stand back, preacher!"

I choked in helpless frustration. "Lord—" I breathed it silently—"You've got the power—can't You stop them?"

The solution was boiling in the lid, and with hands now obviously shaking, Billy pulled the liquid up into the eyedropper. He was ready to shoot. One of the other fellows had loosened his belt, but before he could tighten it as a tourniquet around Billy's arm, Billy was jabbing himself with the needle, missing the vein, jabbing again, and again missing. His whole body was jerking, like a man gone wild. The other two had to grab him, hold him, and guide the needle. Satisfied at last, Billy slumped against the wall, the tension gone from his body and face. He smiled and looked at me.

"Beautiful," he murmured. "It can't do you any harm, Bob. You really ought to try it."

The other two fellows were taking turns shooting up, but I didn't stay to watch them escape on their "high." I tumbled down the stinking stairway as fast as I could in the darkness and didn't stop till I could breathe deeply in the crisp night air outside. I felt unclean, as if I had been on a visit to the devil's forechamber.

The questions were racing through my mind as I walked the trash-littered sidewalks toward our apartment. *Why do they get hung up on that stuff? Why, Lord?* That was the important question.

I knew that we could cure a physical addiction to drugs or to alcohol simply by keeping the body away from the stuff for a certain length of time. That's what they do in hospitals and prisons and rehabilitation centers. The addict or the alcoholic can stay clean as long as he is locked up, without access to his "poison."

But that doesn't solve the real problem—the reason *why* he got hooked in the first place—the emotional frustration, the fear, the guilt, the loneliness, the boredom—whatever is eating away at his soul. As long as the "why" remains, the addict will head for the nearest pusher or bottle sooner or later. It doesn't matter how long he has been clean in a hospital or a prison.

Healing the real problem is the whole point behind Teen Challenge. When an addict comes to us he gets a bath, clean clothes, a bed, three solid meals a day, and a haircut if he needs it; but that won't do him any good unless he experiences something inside himself, unless that thing that hurts deep down inside is healed, and the darkness and restlessness is replaced by light and peace.

Some people classify Teen Challenge as a social agency and our workers as social workers. That isn't quite correct. Though we work with many people whose names are in the files at the police station and the social agencies, our concern is souls, because we believe that's where the real problems lie.

Young people are sick and tired of having religion crammed down their throats. The only way they are going to believe that Jesus Christ has the power to restore their souls, to give them a new life, is to let them see the power and that new life in someone. It can't be faked. It's got to be real. It's had to be real in Ona and in me.

In order to work with addicts and walk the streets telling people about the healing power of Jesus, Ona and I had to spend a lot of time being honest with God and with ourselves. We had to let Him clean out all the little "religious hang-ups" we'd carried around with us, the stuff that could block the channel and make people look at us and wrinkle up their noses and say, "Boy! If that's a Christian, I sure don't need it. If that's all Jesus has done for that guy, I'm sure not going to try it."

As workers with Teen Challenge we had to lead young people in need to the source of power, so that they could hook up with it in their own lives. We were not to cure them or change them; God would do that through Jesus Christ and the Holy Spirit. When the hookup was a real one—and there were addicts who put on phony conversions—the power flowed into their lives and they were set free from the hang-ups that kept them in bondage to drugs. Not only were they free, but they themselves became so filled with the power and light of Jesus that they became His followers and started spreading the good news to others.

That first winter in New York Ona and I spent a lot of time studying the Bible—it's our manual, telling us what to do and how to do it and describing what happens when we've done it or failed to do it.

We also spent a lot of time on our knees. Prayer is the switch that has to be thrown to set the power of God into action. We learned—the hard way—that the success or failure of anything we tried to do was in direct proportion to the prayers that went along with it.

In the early spring we began to ask God earnestly when He wanted us to go to Philadelphia. We had gone down a couple of times to look around the city, and we had talked to a few pastors who seemed anxious to have us minister there.

As Teen Challenge centers are pretty much independent operations, we knew that we would be going to Philadelphia on our own. Nobody would supply us with buildings or funds. We would have to go trusting God. There would be a right time to make the move, a time when God would have prepared the way. And so we waited for His sign.

Ann Wilkerson, David's mother, opened up The Catacomb Chapel, a coffeehouse in Greenwich Village, shortly after our arrival in New York. Mrs. Wilkerson was the woman who had greeted us with a smile the day we arrived at Teen Challenge, and we loved working at the Catacomb with her.

One of the first nights the chapel was open, a tall black boy came in and sat down at a table in the corner. He didn't say a word to any of us. He sat in complete silence, drank his coffee, ate a donut, and just listened. Evening after evening he came. He'd arrive a few minutes after we opened the chapel and would stay till it was time to close. I watched him often, wondering who he was, what he was thinking, why he was there. I could see in his eyes that he was soaking up the conversation around him.

Then one night he came in as usual, but when one of our workers greeted him, he smiled and said "Hello!" He sat at his customary table, but this night he had come to talk. He told us that he had listened, night after night, to the story about Jesus. He had watched us and seen that it was real.

"I want it too," he said simply. And so he bowed his head, and as we prayed with him he turned his life over to God, asked forgiveness for his sins, and invited Jesus to come into his life with light and power.

The boy's name was Bill. We gave him a Bible that night, and from then on he was a friend. Once I mentioned that someday God would send us to Philadelphia. Bill's dark eyes lit up in a smile.

"Maybe," he said, "maybe God will send me too."

IV

ON the way to an appointment one day I decided to have lunch with Ona at the center. She handed me a crumpled newspaper.

"I got it out of the wastepaper basket in the office," she said. "I think you ought to read it."

There in bold type was the headline: "JAIL MY SON! SAVE HIS LIFE!" The news was about a father who had turned his seventeen-year-old son over to the Brooklyn juvenile authorities to keep him from getting killed by drugs.

The newspapers often carried items like this one; yet I felt something special when I read it. Ona was watching me as I read. She didn't say anything, but there was a question in her eyes. I nodded. "Yes, I'll go," I said. "I'll talk to his parents first."

I got the address from the newspaper, and that same afternoon I knocked on the door of the apartment where Danny's parents lived. The woman who opened the door was attractive; yet lines of deep concern had marked her face. Her deep blue eyes were hostile, and at first she was reluctant to let me in. I explained that I was a minister who worked with young people involved with narcotics and that I wanted to visit her son in jail. Shrugging her shoulders in a gesture of resignation, she invited me in.

Danny, she told me, was one of nine children, and for the last several years he had been hopelessly addicted to drugs.

"The first year we didn't know it," she said. "His older brother has a candy store, and Danny stole money from the cash register or cartons of cigarettes from the shelves to support his habit. When we discovered what he was doing, he promised to quit. We believed him, but it was soon evident that he was still on drugs. He was caught breaking and entering into a doctor's office where he tried to steal blank prescription pads. He confessed that he'd been doing this for some time, forging the prescriptions, then buying barbiturates and selling them again to other addicts."

Danny's mother spoke in a monotone, her eyes fastened on mine in a blank, tearless gaze.

"He's been in and out of jail several times," she said. "Each time he promised to stay away from dope. Each time he slipped back in. Sometimes when he was gone from home for a couple of days I walked the streets looking for him. And I've found him lying on the sidewalk, trembling and half-conscious, covered with dirt. We lived in fear that one day he would die. You see, he had rheumatic fever for three years when he was a child, and his heart has been weak ever since. That's why we took him to the judge this time." Moisture filled the mother's eyes, and her knuckles whitened as she clenched and unclenched her hands.

"He'll go to court next week, and they'll decide whether

he'll spend the next three years in the State Reformatory or the State Hospital—" Her voice was grim. She could not allow herself emotion.

"Teen Challenge has helped young people who've been on drugs much longer than your son," I told her. "If Danny wants help I know he can get it."

A fleeting hint of a smile touched her face and was gone. "I pray you are right, Reverend," she said. But I sensed that she could allow herself no hope for her son.

The next day I was allowed to see Danny in prison for ten minutes. He looked like a skinny, defiant young rebel, but he listened to my words almost eagerly.

"Danny," I said, "you know what's ahead of you; you know what kind of a hell you've been living in. There's a power more real than any drug you've ever been high on—it can change you inside—it's Jesus Christ. He changed me. How about it, Danny? If you want it, you can have it. If you want to come to Teen Challenge I will ask the judge to release you into my custody."

There was a new light deep down in Danny's brown eyes. He nodded and looked straight at me. "Yes," he said slowly. "I'd like that."

April 8. I went to court with Danny. Ona and I had prayed that God would have His way with the judge, and I stepped out on that bright spring morning knowing that the case was already settled, that, in fact, God had walked ahead of us every step of the way from the moment He put it into Ona's mind to pick the newspaper out of the wastebasket. Danny didn't know it yet, but God had His hand on him. I whistled as I ran up the courthouse steps.

The judge was impressed by what I had to say about Teen Challenge. He didn't hesitate to put Danny in my custody.

That night Danny came with us to El Bethel Church on Staten Island. He had been raised in the Catholic Church and had never attended this type of service before. He looked around, slightly bewildered at the members of the congregation who clapped their hands vigorously in time with the singing and got down on their knees, praying and praising God in loud voices.

"Danny," I whispered, "remember the power and the peace we talked about, the Jesus Christ who came to set us free?" He nodded. "That's the One they are singing about. That's the One they're talking to in prayer."

Danny watched and listened intently as the preacher talked about the transforming power of Christ. He sat leaning forward in the pew, almost like a young animal ready to leap into flight. When the invitation was given, he ran toward the altar, threw himself down, and began to cry. I followed and knelt beside him.

In between sobs I heard him call out, "Jesus, Jesus, I'm sorry about everything; help me, Jesus, I want to be Yours." I put my hand on his shoulder and thanked God for the answer I knew He had already given to Danny's prayer, the prayer God answers instantly. Danny knew it too. The convulsive sobs were subsiding, Danny was breathing quietly, saying softly over and over again, "Thank you, Jesus, thank you, Jesus." There was a radiant smile on his face, and he looked up with tears streaming.

"It's true, it's true," he said, grasping my hand in his. "I saw a light—everything is different now—Jesus is for real!"

Ona came down to join us; the three of us stood there hugging each other and crying and laughing.

"Wow!" Danny was shaking his head as if he couldn't quite understand it all. "I never even was alive before!"

Back at the center I handed Danny a Bible. "This is where it is," I said. "Sit down and read this book as if every word is truth. It's your survival kit, brother. I've staked my life on it." Danny looked curious as he opened the Book and began to read. It seemed a good time for me to leave him alone then. "If you've got any questions," I told him, "let's talk them over. I'm still learning myself."

Every time I stuck my nose inside the door of the center, there was Danny with his Bible. "Hey, Brother Bartlett, I don't get it. This Jesus, He made dead people come back to life, He fed five thousand people with two little fishes and five loaves of bread, and He walked on the water. And then He told his disciples that when He was gone they were gonna get power to do the same things—" He was plainly puzzled. "I sure don't have any power. I don't get it."

I tried to explain. "Danny, first you've got to believe that Jesus still has this power. Then you've got to believe that this power can move through you."

"Believe, believe," Danny thumped his Bible on the table. "How can you *believe* when you don't? I can't see it, I can't believe it. It's like believing in fairy tales!" I was glad he was being honest with me.

"Didn't something happen to you the other night in church?" I asked him. "Aren't you off drugs?" Danny hung his head.

"Yes, I know about that," he said, "because it happened. But sometimes I get to thinking I'm just making up the whole thing, like I'm not sure I wouldn't go back on drugs if I got out of here."

"Danny," I said sternly, "God saved you because He needs you. Just like He saved all of us here at Teen Challenge to use us. Just like He raised up the money to build this center, like He brought a reporter to write up your story so we could read it in the paper."

When Danny looked at me, there were tears in his eyes. "I want to believe," he said. "You know I do. But what if we're all a bunch of kooks with nothing more than a neat set of positive thinking? What if all of this stuff is just a lot of coincidences?"

I put my hand on Danny's shoulder. "You know what?" I said. "I'm glad you're doubting. And one of these days God is going to prove a few things to you. It says in that Book that if you keep on seeking, you're going to find; if you knock it shall be opened; if you ask you're going to get some answers. And that's the gospel truth!"

Just then Lucy came by in the hallway and waved at us. "Hi, Brother Bartlett; hi, Danny, how's it going?"

Danny shook his head. "I'm kind of having my doubts," he said. "How about you?" Lucy's thin face broke into a wide smile, and she sat on the arm of a chair dangling one skinny leg. Lucy had been at the center for several months. She'd been a heroin addict for years, and when she came to us she looked like a skeleton.

"What's the hang-up today, kid?" her eyes were sympathetic, searching Danny's face, and I thought, *She looks like she cares in a motherly way. Thank you, God. I believe you're going to give Danny some answers already.*

Danny looked at Lucy as if he was wondering whether it

would be worth trying to trust her. Then suddenly he burst out, "I've got to know if there's a real power in Jesus Christ or if it's just us trying to be good, following a set of rules on our own willpower." He settled back in his chair, waiting for her answer. "I don't think I can do it then, not if it's really up to me."

Lucy sat very quietly for a while. When she spoke her voice was low, matter-of-fact.

"Let me tell you what kind of evidence I have," she said. "I was running a shooting gallery in Harlem—you know, where the kids could come in and buy drugs and shoot up. I was a mainliner myself, had been for years. I had asthma real bad, and I couldn't breathe unless I was high on heroin. So you see, I was scared to death to get off the stuff, even if I'd wanted to.

"One night one of my old girl friends brought two new girls to the gallery. She told me they were pushers and that they had better stuff than I had and that it was cheap. So naturally I asked them in. Turned out they were from Teen Challenge. My old girl friend had become a convert. She'd brought the other two to talk to me about Jesus. Man, I got so mad I was gonna throw them out—they were a hazard to my business, and I didn't want any of that Jesus stuff. But something happened that really scared me.

"One of the girls—she was Ona—came over and started talking to me. I'd just come out of the kitchen where I'd taken a shot of heroin. I was flying high and loving it, and I knew the high was gonna last me at least a couple of hours.

"But you know, Ona looked me straight in the eyes—I couldn't turn my eyes away from hers, I tried—and she started talking about Jesus Christ and the power of the Holy Spirit.

Man, I didn't believe any of that stuff, but all of a sudden something real crazy happened. When Ona used the names of Jesus Christ and the Holy Spirit I came off my high. Just like that! I've never been so scared in my life. I mean, I just shot a bunch of chemicals into my vein and I knew it was good stuff, I was already up there on it, and suddenly, boom, I'm down.

"And it wasn't like I was just down. I knew there was another power all around me, keeping me so that I could breathe, and I knew who that power was. Like it was making itself known to me. As if it was saying, 'Look sister, you're feeling the real power now and you've gotta choose. It's Me, or death.'

"A week later I came to the center. I've been off drugs ever since, and the first thing Jesus Christ did when I turned myself over to Him was to cure my asthma."

Danny had listened spellbound. I could tell he knew it was all true.

Lucy stood up and smiled at him. "Since then," she admitted, "I've had to learn to use a lot of willpower to believe that God is doing what He's promised He can do. And sometimes you've got to hang on to that belief in spite of the evidence around you. But don't forget that the real action is God's part. First you believe He's gonna provide a miracle, then He provides it." Lucy patted Danny's Bible. "Go through the book. You find a promise in there that you want to hold onto for yourself, ask God for it, then believe He'll do it, and say thanks. It's bound to happen if you hang in there."

"Thanks, Lucy," Danny was smiling. "I'll try to do my part so He can do His. I'm sorry I got so discouraged. I just got so sick of the way I was thinking and feeling." He placed his hand on the Bible. "I've been reading the Book of Acts," he said. "Those disciples sure did all the things Jesus said they would do—and it all started at Pentecost when they got the power Jesus said He would send them. That's what I'm gonna ask for too—my own personal Pentecost. If everything in here is true, then something will happen."

The next morning I was going to a prayer breakfast sponsored by the Full Gospel Business Men's Fellowship. On an impulse I asked Danny to come along. The meeting was a good one; I enjoyed myself thoroughly; and toward the end, when the speaker asked if anyone wanted to come forward and pray for a spiritual renewal in the city, I went and knelt with the others. When I got up from my knees, Danny was nowhere in sight. For an instant I almost panicked—what if he'd run off? He'd been at the center for only two weeks, and he certainly hadn't made a secret of his doubts about the reality of the power behind the program. My eyes scanned the room again.

Over in a corner a group of men were standing in a circle, obviously praying for someone. I heard loud hallelujahs and "Praise the Lord!" Walking closer, I stood on tiptoe to peer over the men's shoulders. There, in the middle of the circle, was Danny, sitting on a chair, his arms lifted, tears flowing! He was laughing and talking in a language I'd never heard before.

He opened his eyes and saw me. "Praise the Lord, Brother Bartlett!" He leaped up and forced his way through the circle of men to give me a hug. "I just got tuned in to that Pentecostal power you told me about." His face was wet with tears, but he was still laughing.

While I had gone forward to pray, Danny had remained standing, leaning up against the far wall. One of the men had come over and asked him if he had received the Holy Ghost.

"I didn't even know for sure what he was talking about," Danny told me later, "so I said 'no.' He asked me if I wanted it, and I said if it was something Jesus wanted me to have I wanted it. So the man put a chair in the middle of the floor and I sat down. Then a bunch of men started coming toward me from all directions—it was like a Brooklyn rumble, and I didn't know whether to run or stay. The first man explained that what had happened when I first got saved was that I had asked Jesus to come into my life. Now I could ask Him to take over completely. The man told me that if I had anything I needed to repent of, or if I needed to forgive somebody, now was the time to do it. And if I had any hang-ups or doubts or fears between me and Jesus, now was the time to give them up too. That was okay with me. The man said I should tell Jesus I wanted Him to take me and baptize me in the Holy Ghost and then just thank Him and praise Him for it. So I did, and the men laid their hands on me and started praying, and in ten seconds I felt this light and power flow through me, and I was speaking out loud in a language I'd never heard before. It was fantastic!" Danny paused for breath.

"Did it bother you—the speaking in tongues?" I asked him.

"No, but it seemed strange at first, and I was a little worried that maybe I was making it up, except that the more I talked, the more real Jesus Christ seemed to be. I knew He was the One who was pouring this presence over me." Danny looked at me and then down at his hands.

"You know the whole thing was so simple," he said, sounding almost embarrassed. "We try to make something sophisticated out of religion with a bunch of big words. But you know what it felt like when that power was flowing over me?" I shook my head.

"It felt like Jesus was putting His arms around me and just loving me," he went on. "You know, like you imagine a mother or a father really ought to love, or a best buddy. Nothing mystical, no bright vision—just plain love. And I guess I never knew what love felt like before."

I nodded. I knew.

"And what's Jesus telling you to do now?" I felt an odd tightening in my throat. Danny looked up with a smile.

"He's telling me to get with it—to go tell the whole world."

"How would you like to start with Philadelphia?" I asked. But I didn't need to wait for his answer. It was written in the radiance on his face.

V

WE DROVE to Philadelphia in June 1964—Danny, Ona, and I in our small car. Ona was six months pregnant. I had been in touch with a couple of local pastors who had collected enough money from their churches to rent us two small apartments in North Philadelphia, in a section known as the "jungle" for reasons that were very obvious. The buildings were overcrowded and run-down, the streets filthy.

Ten students from Northeast Bible Institute at Green Lane, Pennsylvania, had volunteered to help us the first summer. They arrived the day we moved into our apartments. It got a bit crowded, and Philadelphia had a record heat wave that summer, but God provided us with a couple of signs right off the bat to show us that He was in charge.

Our program for the summer was to hold street meetings and comb the city for young people in need of help. We were also getting acquainted with the churches—to let the Christians know we were in town.

Our first problem was transportation. We couldn't all get

very far in one small car. So that was our first prayer target. "Dear God," we prayed, "You know we need something to travel in, so You must already have provided. Thank You."

A couple of days later two schoolteachers came by to look at our "center." They were Episcopalians and had heard through the grapevine that we were starting a Teen Challenge Center for the rehabilitation of drug addicts. They had been praying for something like that to happen. One of them was working as a counselor in one of the local high schools where student drug addiction was a very serious problem.

"We came by to see what you need," she said.

"A van," I said immediately. I had already gone to a dealer and picked out one on faith. Maybe the schoolteachers would like to contribute a little toward it.

"How much will a van cost?" the teacher asked.

"Twenty-two hundred dollars," I told her. She sat down and wrote out a check. Then she handed it to me. "There you are," she said. I was puzzled by the sound of triumph in her voice. And then I looked at the check. I could hardly believe my own eyes. She had written a check for the whole amount—twenty-two hundred dollars!

Now we had something to travel in—but how would we eat? The only income we had was the personal support Ona and I received from our home churches, plus an occasional contribution from a local church or individual. The ten students had volunteered to work the entire summer without pay and had only pocket money. We expected God to provide our food and shelter. He promised in Matthew 10:9-10 that when the disciples followed His command and went out to preach the Word without bringing money or extra clothes or shoes, they would be given what they needed.

We had prayed, thanking God for His provisions, but we hadn't expected quite all that He had in store for us. A Christian meat-dealer in Delaware called and offered us over three thousand dollars worth of choice beef. We had to rent lockers to store it in. A supply house gave us two hundred cases of canned soup. A bakery began to give us all the bread and pastries we could use. We felt like the Israelites must have felt when it started to rain manna from heaven over the Sinai desert. Already that first summer, farmers from the Delaware Valley began to call us when they had extra produce. All we had to do was go pick it ourselves—tomatoes, lettuce, corn, beans—whatever the season provided.

Every day we walked the streets, handing out tracts and talking to young people. We singled out special trouble areas and held street meetings. That almost got us into big trouble one night.

It was late in the summer and I'd given a big pep talk to our ten students about how we were going to "invade" the black ghetto with the gospel of peace. I really didn't know any better—Philadelphia was new to all of us, and we were exploring areas and methods completely on our own. We didn't have anybody else's mistakes to learn from.

We drove our van into the thick of the black ghetto, parked it, and walked in a group to the steps of an old rundown storefront church. The sidewalk and street were full of people, all of them black, all of them eyeing us.

There we stood on the steps; I was in front, the others were lined up behind me, all of them white. We sang one verse of an old favorite, "There's power in the Blood," and I started yelling through the megaphone.

"Listen all you kids who are lost in drugs, listen all you

girls who sell your bodies . . . listen all you who waste your money on alcohol . . . We've come to tell you about a better way—" I got no further. The people in front of us were backing off, leaving a wide open space for three immaculately dressed black men who were marching directly toward us. They stopped about three feet from us, and casually opened their jackets, exposing three shining guns pointed directly at my stomach. The man in the middle spoke in a smooth, clipped voice.

"White preacher—this is our territory. You've got a choice—be gone or be dead!"

I could tell he meant it. All I could think of was Ona and Danny and those ten kids behind me. I could imagine the headlines the next day: "Street meeting leads to bloody riot." My God, what had I gotten these innocent kids into? Then I felt Ona's steady hand on my shoulder. In a flash I remembered. "Perfect love casteth out fear." We were surrounded by God's love—what did we have to fear?

I managed to smile at the guy who stood facing me.

"We're leaving," I said. "We didn't know this was your territory."

He stepped aside and let us all pass by. The people watched quietly; no one yelled or lifted a hand after us. And soon we were safely home.

I didn't know it then, but I found out later, that we'd invaded the territory of the Black Muslims! That isn't done without someone getting hurt—unless God goes before and protects.

Why didn't He just keep us from going in the first place? Maybe to teach us a lesson. Now we knew the score. We knew what wouldn't work. And we knew what to pray for.

God has sent black brothers and sisters to our center since then. And they have carried the message back to the black ghetto.

One night Danny and I were walking down Montgomery Avenue. We decided to stop in at the 17th District Police Station. The narcotics officer was there, and we introduced ourselves and told him what Teen Challenge was all about.

The officer listened patiently, but it was obvious that he thought we were wasting our time trying to help addicts.

"All you can do is put them in jail to protect the rest of society," he said.

Danny stepped forward and leaned on the officer's desk.

"I was on drugs for several years," he said. "I was in and out of jail and at last my parents gave up on me and committed me to the judge. I was going to be sent to th. Reformatory or the State Hospital for three years. Instead I was cured."

The officer looked at Danny with obvious interest.

"What do you mean 'cured'?" he asked. "Medical science hasn't been able to develop a cure yet. The Federal Hospital for Drug Rehabilitation in Lexington, Kentucky, claims they've got two percent success with their patients—and I doubt if it's that much. How do you mean, you're cured?"

"I mean I'm cured. All at once, all of a sudden. And I haven't had any since, haven't ever wanted any again. And I work with addicts—I'm around the stuff all the time, every day." Danny's testimony rang true and the officer listened with new interest.

We told him about the Teen Challenge program in New York where the cure percentage is 80–85%, and how we had been led to open a center in Philadelphia.

By the time we were ready to go, the officer had promised us all the help and cooperation his department could give.

Leaving the police station we saw two teen-age girls standing on the corner. Their eyes were blurred and their lips dry and cracked. They were obviously high. We gave them a booklet about the Teen Challenge program and watched as they looked at it, laughed, and threw it into the gutter. Danny cringed.

"I wish we could just touch them with our hands and they would be delivered from that hell," he said. "But I know they've got to want it."

We were spending more and more time down around Rittenhouse Square where the hippies and the drug addicts congregated every evening. The area reminded me of Washington Square in New York, and one day Ona told me that she felt we ought to look for a place to open a coffeehouse.

That night all of us prayed that God would show us the way. We also prayed that He would lead us to the right place, and that He would keep us from making a mistake.

"Open the doors you want us to go through, God, and close the ones You don't want us to go through—even if you have to slam them in our faces." I'd prayed that kind of prayer before and gotten a pretty sore nose when I'd gone ahead on my own steam, following my own inclinations. I had to learn to take my prayers as seriously as I wanted God to take them.

The next couple of days I drove up and down the streets around Rittenhouse Square and found absolutely nothing. Yet I felt that God really wanted us to open up a coffee shop.

"If you're trying to show me, Lord, You've got to make it plain; I just don't seem to get any direction." I was driving down a deserted side street while I was praying, and I stopped the car halfway down the street. There was nothing there that would attract any trade, just a few stores that were closed for the evening. I looked up and down the street, and then my eyes fell on the building directly across from where I'd stopped. There, in a basement window, was a crudely lettered handwritten sign: "FOR RENT." "You must be kidding, Lord," I protested. "Nobody comes down this street." But there was the sign, and it was the only one I'd seen around.

I drove Ona by to look at the place. We had to walk down from the street and duck into a long narrow room. It was a filthy mess, but Ona liked it immediately. If God wanted us there, the least we could do was try to fix it up.

But I wasn't too sure. I hated to put out money for rent on a place nobody could find. So I said, "Lord, You promised to close the door and You didn't, so we came marching through it. But I sure wish You'd give me another sign of some sort." It was to come sooner than I might imagine.

We paid the rent; the place was officially ours. That night we sat around in the apartment and talked about how we could fix it up. A knock came on our door. I opened it, and there stood Bill, our old friend from the coffeehouse in New York. He was grinning all over.

"Hi!" he said. "I came to help—do you have a coffee shop yet?" My mouth must have fallen open. Surely Bill was my sign.

God had sent him, there was no doubt in my mind about that. He moved into the center and stayed with us for several months, helping wherever he was needed. Bill was an artist, and he painted the walls of our coffee shop. The background color was dark brown; we hung burlap under the ceiling and set up several tables. There was a small kitchen in the back so we could serve coffee or tea and donuts. We called the place Hidden Manna. It was certainly hidden away, and what we offered there was the Bread of Life for those who had eyes to see.

We need not have worried about getting customers. On one of our first weekends, another friend from New York dropped in, a friend who had not become a convert. Joe nearly fell backward out the door when he first saw us.

"What are you guys doing here?" he asked in astonishment.

We told him we had just opened up, and he wanted to know if we were looking for customers. "Sure," we said, and Joe ducked back out the door and was gone for half-an-hour. He returned with what seemed like half the kids from the Square. He was like that. Joe was the kind of guy who drew other people like the Pied Piper.

"How come you bring them here?" I asked Joe. "You don't believe in the stuff we're talking about." Joe looked at the tables surrounded by kids eagerly talking about their favorite subject: Christ. On the tables, amid coffee cups and donut crumbs, were open Bibles.

"You just keep talking, preacher," he said. "Who knows what I might believe one day."

Joe kept coming for months, and every night he drew the crowds. But he was also falling in love, and we looked at his situation with growing concern. Joe was thirty-five with an ex-wife and a child somewhere. He was divorced, and now Joe wanted to marry an eighteen-year-old drug addict.

"If I accept Jesus Christ, I have to get married by a preacher, right? God would want me to, wouldn't He?" I nodded and he continued. "But God might not want me to marry Rosie."

"Joe," I told him, "God has to come before anybody or anything. You have to give your life to Him first. I can't tell you what you can or cannot do. That will be between you and God."

Joe looked thoughtful. Then he shook his head sadly. "I don't know, Brother Bartlett, I just don't know."

We talked about it several times. Sometimes there would be tears in Joe's eyes. He was torn by the dilemma—Rosie or Jesus—and he cried over both.

In the end he turned away. The last we heard he was arrested for giving a party with minors present where there was alcohol and drugs. Joe—

In the meantime our street changed. Over the months after we opened Hidden Manna, the whole street had become Main Street for art galleries, antique shops, and way-out shops. God had led us to the most strategic location in the entire Rittenhouse Square area!

In the fall of 1964 we held a big rally in the Philadelphia Gospel Temple. Teen Challenge was becoming known. Addicts were coming for help; we were known by local agencies and authorities who referred parents and kids in trouble to us. It was obvious that we needed larger quarters than our two small, crowded apartments.

"I'm going to look for a big house someplace," I told Ona, and in my mind I had visions of an old mansion, something like the one David Wilkerson had in New York. As I drove through the Germantown area one bright beautiful day, there it was—exactly what I'd dreamed about. The house was perfect in every way. Just what we needed, and surrounded by large, beautiful grounds. The rally and contributions from several sources would provide the money for a down payment. The only snag was the zoning. We would have to get special permission from the zoning board to operate our center there.

"Don't worry," I said to Ona and Danny. "You know the Lord is going to let us have that house." I was so sure of the outcome that I made announcements to the churches and organizations that supported us.

"We'll move in after Christmas," I said. "And we'll have a dedication ceremony that will long be remembered." I was already envisioning a great celebration.

Ona has a way of hanging caution signs before me when I start getting too sure of myself, but this time I knew that God was on my side.

We were planning to spend Christmas in Oklahoma with Ona's parents. They hadn't seen their new grandson yet. Danny would go with us, and I was looking forward to telling our home church about our success in Philadelphia.

"They were the first ones to believe in us, remember, honey?" I reminded Ona.

I was going to speak at a meeting in our church one evening during the holiday season. I was preparing the triumphant message when Ona called me to the phone. Long distance from Philadelphia. The Germantown Zoning Board had just met and turned our application down.

At first I wanted to cry. Then I got furious and stormed up and down our room while Ona sat quietly watching me.

"That's the end of it," I fumed. "Those ungrateful people, turning us down when we're trying to help their kids. I'll never go back there again." I threw myself on the bed and looked at Ona. "Say something," I sputtered. "Don't just sit there."

"I'll say something if you'll listen," Ona said softly. "Can you forget about your own hurt pride for a minute and remember who called us to Philadelphia in the first place? Do you think a silly old zoning board could have turned us down if God had really picked that house for us?"

"Good Lord," I groaned. "I did it again. I ran so far ahead of God I couldn't even hear Him yelling at me to stop."

Ona leaned down and kissed me on the nose.

"Don't worry, honey," she said. "As long as your nose can take your running up against slamming doors, God will keep you humble."

VI

BACK in Philadelphia we had our problem still with us. What do we do about a building? Our two small apartments just wouldn't do any longer. We all got to our knees in the living room and began to pray. We knew that prayer isn't just talking to God, letting Him know what we want. Prayer is listening to what He wants us to do. At Teen Challenge we do a lot of praying, and sometimes our sessions last for hours—even all through the night. We call it "praying through."

How do we know when we've prayed "through"? First we tell God our problem. Not lightly, from the top of our heads, because then it's not really a problem and God knows that. But we look at that problem until we really feel a burden about it, until we could cry about it, and know in our hearts that we want desperately for God to do something. And that's when something begins to happen. There, on our knees, we begin to see our problem from a different angle. And we begin to see ourselves as God sees us and know something in us may be blocking His solution to our problem. That's when we really feel like crying.

That's when we cry out, "Oh God, take away whatever it is in me that is blocking You. Forgive me, God." This is the prayer of repentance, and with it always comes forgiveness.

We've learned that the prayer of repentance isn't just for sinners who've never accepted Christ. It is for all of us who've turned our lives over to God and tuned in to His presence— and then turned away like Peter. He was one of Jesus' most trusted disciples, and he fell flat on his face a couple of times. He even denied that he *knew* Jesus. It says in the Bible that when the cock crowed Peter went out and cried bitterly. Those were tears of repentance. If he hadn't repented, he couldn't have been forgiven. It's as simple as that, a spiritual law, as binding as any law in nature. I expect an apple to fall to the ground if I drop it. I expect God's forgiveness when I ask it. That's just as dependable as the law of gravity.

"Praying through" is simply tuning in to God and staying with it till we've seen what's been blocking the channel, and we've let Him take the block away by repenting of it. Then we know the peace of God, and this time we cry tears of gratitude and joy. Somehow, the whole problem we were so worried about has dissolved itself. Paul writes about that in his letter to the Philippians 4:6–7. He says not to worry about anything, but to tell God everything you need with a thankful heart, and the peace of God which is far beyond human understanding will keep your hearts and minds safe in Christ.

That is a great promise. We depend upon it during our "praying through" times at Teen Challenge. It often happens that before God can give some of us peace, we have to confess a few things and forgive each other for wrong attitudes we've held. Wrong attitudes can sure hold up the works.

That particular night Ona had to confess to being a little disgusted with my cocksure attitude about the mansion in Germantown. Who could really blame her? God showed me a nice long list of hang-ups of my own—like impatience, pride, conceit, a quick temper, and most of all, a lack of trust in Him and His ability to lead us.

I had to confess all these sins and ask forgiveness. When God's peace descended upon our valiant little band of prayer warriors, we shouted for joy, and all fear and tension about the future was gone.

The next few days I honestly forgot all about the pressing need for a building and went on about my daily business, which by now included a growing number of appearances before schools and organizations who wanted to work with us.

We had several converts, former drug addicts, and workers living in the two apartments, girls in one and boys in the other. I kept getting letters and calls from other young people who wanted to join our staff. Earlier I had said we just couldn't take in any more addicts or workers, but now I confidently said, "Come on. The Lord is getting us a bigger place. He knows we need it." And I believed it.

Driving down the main street of Philadelphia one day, all of a sudden I felt impressed to stop. I pulled over to the curb, then looked up and down the street wondering what in the world I was doing there. I was about one block from Temple University on North Broad Street, a main thoroughfare with office buildings and stores. I knew that just beyond Broad Street was the black ghetto. It was the kind of neighborhood I would try to avoid if I was going to set up a place to rehabilitate drug addicts.

My eyes were drawn to the building directly across from me. It was a four-story, narrow brownstone squeezed in between a jewelry store and used furniture store on one side, and an office building on the other. It looked considerably more dilapidated than its neighbors, and it had a "FOR SALE" sign on it. I noticed that funny fluttery feeling in my stomach and shook my head. "Oh, no, Lord," I sighed. "You wouldn't." The funny feeling grew stronger. "Or would You?" Maybe God knew something about the building that I didn't know. Maybe it had a beautiful garden in the back; maybe it was furnished exactly to suit our needs. I knew better than to disregard the sensation I felt inside. I'd tried picking my own location before.

"Okay, Lord," I said. "I'll call the number on the sign and see if anybody wants to show me the place. But if this isn't of You, Lord, You'd better keep someone from answering when I call."

There was a phone booth on the next corner. I pulled over, dialed the number, and a man answered immediately, as if he'd been waiting.

I told him who I was and that I'd like to see the building sometime, if it was convenient.

"Stay where you are," the man said. "I'll come right down."

There was no way to get out of it. I met the man on the doorstep of 1620 North Broad, and my heart fell when he opened the door. The building belonged to a fraternity at the University and it looked as if they had kept pigs in it. Filth and empty beer cans were everywhere. The place looked utterly unfit for human habitation. There was no beautiful garden in the back; the building went all the way to the alley; and the rooms were helter-skelter, painted in crazy colors with wallpaper torn to shreds and ceiling tiles buckling and falling down. One huge room on the first floor had a big hole in the floor. The man said something about an indoor swimming pool. Whatever the hole had been, it now served as an enormous receptacle for trash.

The more I saw of the place, the sicker I got; yet for all my inward grumblings I got only one answer. God was saying very plainly, "This is the building."

I couldn't help arguing. "But how are we going to clean it? Where do we get the money to remodel? Surely, God, You can see this is no place to rehabilitate drug addicts. Besides, it stinks!"

Deep down within me the voice kept saying, "This is the building." I was defeated.

"How much?" I asked the man.

"Forty-five thousand dollars," he said. It was far too much, and I made a counteroffer, testing God.

"How about twenty-five thousand?" I asked recklessly. The man looked at me without blinking an eye.

"Yes, I think we can go as low as that," he replied.

Good grief, I thought. *What do I do now?*

"I can't give you a down payment for another two weeks," I said, hoping that would not be satisfactory. "How about five thousand dollars down then?" I didn't know where the five thousand dollars would come from, and I held my breath, wondering how far out on a limb God was going to let me go.

"Fine," the man agreed. "Let's draw up the papers."

The whole episode had taken maybe half-an-hour, and I

called Ona to tell her God had found us a building. She gasped and said, "I bet it's perfect for our needs."

We were to take possession of the building in a couple of weeks, and I used the time to recruit young people from the churches around the city to help on the cleanup job. Five boys from the University were still living in the building, and apparently they decided to throw one last giant party before moving out. When we arrived with scrub brushes and buckets and an army of kids from churches in the area, we walked into a mess that made me think the building had been clean when I first saw it. I almost sent the kids home again. Beer cans, used prophylactics, and vomit covered the floor of every room in the building. Urine and vomit stains splattered the walls. The stench was overwhelming.

"Okay, God." I said it out loud. "We're claiming this place for You. Please go ahead of us and cover every room with the Blood of Jesus and fill it with Your Holy Spirit. Thank you."

Some of our staff workers got busy collecting the trash into huge barrels and the rest of us went to work with scrub brushes and disinfectants.

Toward the end of the day Ona and I walked through the building. The trash and the stench were gone. We could hear kids singing from one end of the house to another, "Onward Christian Soldiers."

The place still looked a mess. Paint was peeling off the walls; stairs were broken; some of the old wooden doors wouldn't close—there was much to be done yet. The floor plan made no sense. Some walls would have to come down and others go up. We didn't have the money, the materials, or the skills to do the job. We were bone-tired, but I could feel a growing excitement about our new headquarters. God had picked it, and I was beginning to see His point. I squeezed Ona's hand, and she looked up at me, smiling, with smudges of dirt on her nose and on her cheeks.

This wasn't exactly the kind of future I had dreamt about offering her; yet I knew that neither of us would want to exchange places with anyone anywhere. Ona must have read my thoughts. She giggled and stood on tiptoe to lean her head on my shoulder.

"Isn't it exciting?" she marveled. "Nobody but God would pick an impossible place like this to make a perfect Teen Challenge Center. I can't wait to see how He's going to do it!"

We moved in the very next day. All our belongings were piled in the van, and we put the boys in one end of the new building and the girls in the other. There wasn't much furniture. We had some bunk beds and a few dressers, and that was about it. God had showed us His miracle power from the beginning, but He didn't give us what we needed all finished and wrapped up. He provided plywood and boards, hammer, nails, and saw, so that our boys could build tables and benches for the dining room. A contractor donated paint. We did the work.

I gathered our small band of workers in the first floor front room, which I called my "office," and pointed to a stack of papers and letters on my desk.

"We're going to have to pray," I said. "God has given us a house. We're going to pray for finances and furnishings and food, and we're going to pray that He will bring the workers He knows we need. I've got a bunch of letters from kids who want to join our staff, and I have invitations to speak at rallies and in Bible colleges. We've got to pray that God will pick the workers. I wouldn't know what to look for."

Patti, a tall brunette from Kansas who had been with us for several months, spoke up. "Pray for me, Brother Bartlett," she said. "Pray that God will show me the job He wants me to do and that He'll teach me how to do it."

The others nodded and murmured agreement, and Danny cleared his throat. I caught his glance before he quickly bowed his head and stared at the floor. I knew that something was bugging Danny, and I could only guess what it was. He had been with us for nearly a year now, and I felt certain that God was beginning to nudge him about preparing for a special job. I had prayed that he would go to a Bible college, but Danny had never gone beyond the seventh grade and was very self-conscious about that. "You show him, Lord," I prayed under my breath. "He can go through Bible college with flying colors when You lead him."

We joined hands in a circle and prayed for God to meet our needs, to send the workers who could cook and build and paint, work in the office, with the converts, and on the streets. "And Lord," I heard Billy pray, "please send someone who can play the trumpet!"

As winter melted into sloshy spring, our center began shaping up. Some of us who had never handled a hammer or a saw or a paintbrush learned all about it, and when we got into a tight squeeze, God always sent someone who knew how to handle the situation. A contractor agreed to do some outside work on the front of the building and didn't hedge when I told him we were short on cash and had to rely on gifts to meet our bills. One day he asked one of our girls to give him a tour of the center. She took him all through the building. In the kitchen she opened the pantry door, and he saw the shelves were gaping empty. That morning we had used the last of our oatmeal, and we had gathered in the chapel confident that God would provide food by lunchtime.

The contractor looked from the girl to the empty shelves and back to the girl, who was smiling. "God never lets us down," she assured him. "Don't you worry." She was thinking of the bill we owed the man already.

"I'm not worried," the contractor said as he reached into his back pocket and brought out his wallet. "Here, go get some lunch!" He handed her a crisp hundred dollar bill and walked off.

I traveled from campus to campus that spring, speaking to crowds of young people about our work. Always there were large groups who came to talk about working with us in Philadelphia. Some were obviously romantic crusaders, eager to win the world for God. Others were dissatisfied and bored with school or staying at home. I wondered how long it would take them to get tired of fighting rats and cockroaches, sleeping on lumpy mattresses, and working long hard hours on bologna sandwiches, tomato soup, and powdered milk.

Yet, I knew that God would select a team of workers from among the eager young students who came to talk. God had recruited us that way, less than two years before. Had I been as unfit for my job then as some of these volunteers seemed to be?

In a small college in Maine I met Richard. After the meeting he told me that he had arrived too late to hear a word of what had been said, but that God had told him to come to Teen Challenge. Richard's hair was neatly combed, his suit was of the latest cut and style, and I thought I got a whiff of an expensive men's cologne. I looked at his hands. They didn't look as if they'd done much hard labor.

"What can you do?" I asked. Richard smiled and shrugged his shoulders.

"I just know I'm supposed to come," he said. "I'm sure I can do just about anything."

I wanted to groan, but Richard continued. "I'm a music major, and I can lead a choir and play the piano and organ."

That's just great! I thought. *We don't have a choir, we don't have an organ, and our old upright piano came with the building. Half the keys aren't working.*

"Why don't you fill in an application?" I said. "Maybe you can come as a summer worker, if God so leads."

Richard frowned. "There's only one problem," he said. "I really can't promise just when I can come. My grandmother is sick, and I don't feel I can leave as long as she is that way." He smiled and grasped my hand. "But I'll fill in an application and call to let you know when I'm available."

I said "Fine!" and watched him walk confidently out of the chapel. *Good Lord,* I thought. *How can a guy like that come to work in the ghetto? Why didn't I just tell him to forget it?* Suddenly I remembered the verse in the Bible where it says that men look at the outward appearance while God looks at the heart. Had God really picked Richard for Teen Challenge? It didn't make sense. I shrugged. "Okay, Lord," I said, "if You picked him, You bring him. I won't tell him he can't come. But if You didn't pick him, Lord, please stop him."

In Camden, New Jersey, a tall girl came up to me after a rally. "I'm Sunday Bachman," she told me. "I think the Lord wants me to come to Teen Challenge. I want to find out for sure." There was a steady searching look in her eyes, and I knew she was serious.

"What do you do?" I asked.

"I work in the business office of an oil company," she replied. "I worked in a bank for several years. I make pretty good money now, and I want to be sure about this thing. I don't want to leave a good job to come and work for nothing if it isn't the Lord's will."

Sunday was looking at me, and I knew she was waiting for something. Suddenly I remembered Billy's prayer in my office a couple of months earlier.

"This may sound silly," I said. "But we've been praying for someone who can play a trumpet—and we do need an office worker."

I watched Sunday's eyes light up and fill with tears.

"I love to play the trumpet," she said quietly. "I've been praying about this decision and every so often I would think about playing my trumpet at a Teen Challenge meeting." She laughed then, all indecision gone. "I just got a raise at the office, and I have a brand new car. I have some debts, and I really can't afford to quit. The Lord is going to have to take care of all that."

"He will," I said. "If He wants you to come, He can take care of all the practical details." I didn't need to tell her that —she knew it already.

The day Sunday arrived at Teen Challenge we were almost out of food again. She came in time for lunch—tomato soup and bologna sandwiches. When she sat down to eat, the rickety old chair broke under her. She smiled bravely as we explained that this happened on an average of once a meal, but that we were praying for new chairs—and a variety of soups.

After lunch I showed her the "business office," an old desk with a squeaky chair which she tested carefully before sitting down.

She glanced quickly at our ledger—our balance at the bank was under ten dollars at the time, but I explained that we really didn't have a thing to worry about. Money always came in before our debts became overdue. She looked at me and winked.

"I see," she said. "My job is to set up a budget based on what we need, not on what we have, and then to pray in the money."

"Right," I answered. "We can't make a budget on what we have, because then we couldn't have a budget. It really is a lot easier than having to worry about staying within a set income."

Sunday leaned back in her chair and started laughing. She laughed till tears came in her eyes. Then she shook her head and looked at me.

"I don't know what I'm doing here," she said. "Everything I've ever learned in the bank and in the oil company about sound money management tells me you're absolutely out of your minds. The whole thing is so impossible that I'm either going to have to learn to trust God completely or go nuts worrying." She sat up straight in her chair and said briskly, "I guess God brought me here because He knew I needed to learn how to trust Him."

VII

THE God Squad didn't happen overnight. There were times I thought it wouldn't happen at all. That was when I got to planning and anticipating and running ahead of God. The workers were coming, but not always in the packages I expected. When I saw the building God had chosen for us I wanted to run the other way. So it was with some of the workers. I thought surely they couldn't be the ones God had picked, or if they were, then *He* must have made a mistake.

Of course I realized that there was no way a worker could come to us already trained for the job. Our work is highly unpredictable in that God opens unexpected doors of opportunity for new ministries, and we are always dealing with people whose problems and needs can be met only on an individual basis.

We are as strict in selecting workers as we are in admitting addicts to our center. We have learned by experience that an addict has to be dead serious about wanting help—he must be willing to give up his old habits and hang-ups in order to get rid of the shackles of addiction.

We tell the addict in advance that it won't be easy, that the going will be rough sometimes, and he'll want to slip back into the old way of life. That's when he will have to be prepared to take the discipline of hard rules; that's when willpower comes into the picture, the stubborn determination not to give up.

Our workers have to be equally determined. They, too, must submit to self-discipline and rigid rules. We have learned the hard way that unless the workers live by the rules, we can't expect the new converts to learn. We can't have double standards and expect them to believe in us—or in the power and presence of Jesus Christ in our lives.

Our workers are provided with a place to sleep and three meals a day. When we first started the center our workers received a small monthly salary, just enough to pay for toothpaste and other necessities. But about a year after we opened our center, we hit a financial crisis, and it looked pretty desperate. The prayer chain had been going around the clock for several days, but the amounts we received in the mail and at local church services and rallies were minimal, much smaller than usual. It was at the end of the summer season; our summer workers were still with us. They were students from Bible colleges all over the country, and would be returning to school in another couple of weeks.

We were all gathered in the chapel at the main center. Some of us had prayed there through the night. The situation was desperate; in fact, if we didn't come up with two thousand dollars before the day was over, the bank would take our building.

I stood up in front of the chapel and looked over the rows of faces before me. There were about sixty of us that morning, former addicts and workers. I saw tears and the look of helplessness and deep concern as they looked at me—I was their leader. We had come this far—was it the end?

A wave of utter helplessness flowed over me. "Oh God," I cried aloud, "search us and see if there be anything hidden in our hearts to block You. Our needs are known; we want only to serve You and live to Your glory." I was crying openly, and could hear the sobs from my co-workers. "Help us, God; help us to trust You even when everything looks hopeless."

A stillness settled over our little chapel, and within myself I felt a new peace. Somehow I knew that God was answering our prayers; that, in fact, He had already answered them.

I looked up to see one of the summer workers standing in the pew. Tears were streaming down his face, and there was a glow over his smile. "Brother Bartlett," he said, "God has just shown me that I haven't trusted Him to take care of my needs. I've been saving my money to go back to school. I know I'm supposed to give that money to you, and God will provide for my tuition. I've got two hundred dollars."

A girl jumped up in the front of the chapel. "God's been talking to me, too," she said, laughing and crying both at once. "I've got eighty dollars saved for my tuition. God says for me to give it and learn to trust Him."

I could hardly believe my own ears. One after another they stood up and turned their savings, their last pennies, over, rejoicing and praising God in the process.

Harold, a regular staff member, had been kneeling near the back of the chapel. I had seen his body shake with sobs. Now he slowly came to his feet and raised his hand to get my attention. Harold was a slow talker and seldom spoke up in chapel. But something was heavy on his mind.

"Do you have something to share, Brother Harold?" I beckoned for him to come forward. He walked up the aisle, and beside the altar he turned to face the group, which was now standing, many of them softly crying or praying with arms raised.

Harold sighed deeply and began to speak haltingly. "I can only share what God is telling me to do," he said. "I've always been a penny pincher and a worrier about money. Maybe it's because I never had much at home." Harold's parents were hard-working Mennonite farmers. He had worked to put himself through school in the hopes of one day becoming a college teacher. He had wandered into our Hidden Manna Coffeehouse one day, and later God had spoken to him about coming to Teen Challenge as a worker. I had my reservations—he seemed too slow and quite preoccupied with philosophy and intellectual religion. He just didn't seem like the Teen Challenge type.

How wrong I had been in my evaluation! I stood watching him there in the chapel and quietly thanked God who knew Harold so much better than I. Who could have guessed that Harold with his love of books and philosophies would turn out to be a sheer genius with a hammer and nails, with wiring, with plumbing, and with a paintbrush? Who but God?

The workers and the ex-drug addicts were watching and listening intently as Harold continued talking. "God's telling me to quit accepting a salary from Teen Challenge and to begin trusting Him for my support." There was a moment of utter silence before a loud chorus of "Praise God," and "Thank you, Jesus," broke out. Ona and I stood quietly watching as other regular staff workers came to join Harold in his decision to rely completely on God for finances.

That day was a memorable one in many ways. For one thing, when we added up the money our workers had donated, it came to exactly two thousand dollars.

In a staff meeting later, it became clear that God had made Himself very real to all of our workers that day. In giving up the security of a salary, however small, they had literally put themselves into God's hands in a new way; and it seemed as if God, in turn, had given each of them a greater feeling of joy and faith. We decided to take God's strong hint and made it a policy at the center not to offer a salary to workers. That way it would be obvious that no one came to join our staff to find security. It would take dedication, courage, and faith to become a full-time staff worker at our center, and we trusted that God wanted exactly those qualities in His Squad members.

We hadn't realized what an impression this would make on the drug addicts who came to the center for help.

Carlos, a twenty-three-year-old Puerto Rican who had been addicted to heroin for several years, had come to us from jail. He was a moody fellow with a quick temper, and he'd already caused trouble in the boys' dorm. For Carlos there was a choice between Teen Challenge and going back to jail, and so far he was considering us as the lesser of two evils.

I had told him that unless he submitted to our program— and that meant trusting Jesus all the way and turning from his old habits—he would have to leave. Carlos looked at me with dark brooding eyes and shook his head. "I don't dig this Jesus," he said. "You people are just too religious for me."

Carlos was in the chapel that morning when the workers

gave their savings and their salaries. He heard their confessions of selfishness and lack of trust in God and saw their obvious joy and relief when they had given their all to God.

That night at our regular chapel service he came to the altar during the first hymn! "Pray for me, Brother Bartlett," he shouted. "I thought you people were a bunch of religious nuts, and I never believed you when you said that Jesus loves me and that you love me too—" Tears were streaming down his face, and he fell to his knees before the altar. "If you people come here to work with junkies like me without getting paid for it, I know Jesus has got to be real. I want Him to be real for me too!"

It is part of the story that our mail showed a marked increase in contributions the very next day. God had led us through a dry spell for an obvious purpose.

We sometimes prayed for workers who could do a specific job, and God invariably sent us the raw material, not the finished product. Sometimes He brought us workers who thought they had been called to do a specific job—and when God had done His part in molding and working on their hearts and minds, they discovered that they were able to face challenges and tasks that would have sent them running home a few months earlier.

I've met young people at meetings across the country who have told me wistfully, "I wish I had the faith and the ability to be a Teen Challenge worker." I always have to smile. None of us came ready-made, either with faith or with ability to do God's work. Faith and ability are qualities that develop with use. The only qualification for being used by God is to be willing to let God make the necessary changes in us.

I like to think of it this way. God opens a door marked "Opportunity." We walk through it and see that on the other side it is marked "Responsibility." Every one of us at Teen Challenge has had to learn what responsibility means. It didn't come easy to any of us. We've made mistakes that were costly.

It has also happened that we've welcomed workers on our staff who couldn't take it. They lacked the willpower to discipline themselves and stick it out when things got a little rough. When that happens the addicts in our program suffer the most.

We once had a staff worker who thought our rules were too strict. She sympathized with a girl convert who wanted to have a weekend pass in order to see her addict husband on the outside. In the end, the staff worker took matters into her own hands and walked out with the convert. Unfortunately the girl went back on heroin, and feeling she had failed, our staff worker quit the program for good.

Thank God this doesn't happen often. Workers don't come to Philadelphia on the spur of the moment. Having to raise their own support before they come is sure to weed out adventurers.

Still, I pray a lot before asking anyone to join our staff. Peg was one of the few workers I was really excited about when she submitted her application. She was a college graduate and had been a salaried legal secretary for a couple of years. I thought God had really picked the perfect secretary for me. Her papers showed that she was an excellent typist; she could take shorthand and operate all kinds of office machinery. Those were the early days when our office machines consisted of Ona's aging portable typewriter, but I couldn't resist the vision of a streamlined operation.

I couldn't wait for Peg to join us, and I knew God's hand was in it. Peg had asked for some time to settle some debts and sell her new car—she called it getting rid of her "hang-ups"—but she had confessed there was one hang-up she didn't want to get rid of—her piano. Could she bring it? Could she! We had been praying for a piano for some time, because music is so much a part of our life at Teen Challenge. We'd been getting along with the old upright with missing keys—and my tambourine—but still, we felt certain God would provide something better.

Shortly after we heard about Peg's piano, I had a long-distance phone call from Maine. It took a moment before I recognized the voice at the other end. It was Richard, the music major. "Brother Bartlett, I'm ready to come." He sounded enthusiastic. "I'll be there in two weeks."

It looked as if God was working overtime.

I almost reversed my thinking about Peg when she arrived. She was cute, and she knew it. She was bright, and it was obvious that she knew that too. She was an incessant talker, and the first day at the center she managed to wander into the boys' lounge three times.

Ona took her aside and explained our rules. Girls don't talk to boys except when business makes it necessary. Among the converts the rule is absolute—no fraternization whatsoever.

Peg giggled and said she forgot. She was sorry and it wouldn't happen anymore. Fifteen minutes later she wandered into the boys' lounge again.

Without question Peg was the fastest and most efficient

secretary I'd ever seen—when she worked, that is. She would perform with the efficiency and punctuality of a computer for three solid weeks—and then fool around for the next three weeks letting papers pile high on her desk. She would always have legitimate—if strange—excuses. Once I wanted to dictate a few letters and she was nowhere to be found in the building. After an extensive search, someone happened to look out the back door, and there was Peg, covered with grease and oil, in the process of fixing the carburetor on one of our cars.

Peg had many talents: she could sing, play the piano, cook, sew, fix broken-down cars or radios; she was a wonderful office worker, quick-witted with a sense of humor. But she had no self-discipline whatsoever. She would throw a temper tantrum at the least provocation and would run out of the room, slamming the door if her feelings got hurt.

This situation could not go on. Ex-addicts who have just come off drugs are sensitive and need all the steady assurance they can get. Having a staff worker throw a temper tantrum could be like lighting a fuse to a keg of dynamite. Peg would have to grow up—or leave.

Ona and I talked about it, and prayed. We were as concerned for Peg as we are about any addict who comes to us. For the addict it is so obviously a matter of life or death. Yet this girl's uncontrolled emotions had her in bondage too, and only a deeper relationship with Christ could set her free.

Peg's first step toward freedom from self came at the altar in the chapel. That's where we found her one morning with eyes swollen red from tears, but sparkling with a new light.

"Oh, Sister Bartlett," she cried. "I thought I was a Christian when I came here, but it was only surface. I've been such a mess. Can you forgive me?"

"Of course we forgive you," Ona said. I watched the two young women hug each other. "Jesus forgives us all." Ona smiled through tears.

Peg looked suddenly doubtful. "But do you think I'll ever really learn?" she asked.

"Of course you will." Ona took both of her hands and held them. "The secret of self-control is to let Jesus have control. You stick with Him; He'll handle your emotions. He sure took care of mine."

Peg brightened. "I didn't know you had problems like that," she said, and Ona laughed.

"We all have hang-ups, and without Jesus in control I'd probably still be the most frightened girl in all of Oklahoma."

Ona explained to Peg that giving Jesus Christ the right to control her emotions was like being cured of the emotional hang-up on drugs. From now on it would be a matter of overcoming the habit of reacting in the old way. "You overcome the old habit by replacing it with a new pattern," she said, "and in the beginning it isn't easy. It takes a lot of prayer and a lot of plain determination. The Bible tells us to let God renew our minds from within, to let the mind which is in Christ be in us; and that's what has to happen in order for Christ to really live in us and have control over our lives."

Peg looked as if she was trying hard to grasp all that Ona said. "Wow!" she exclaimed. "That sounds hard. I don't know if I can do it."

"You can't," Ona continued, "not by yourself, and that's the whole point. Your mind and your emotions have been filled with self-pity and self-admiration and quick temper and envy and confusion and restlessness, and you haven't had a bit of peace or joy or love. Now you just let go and let that love and joy and peace come through you instead. Jesus Christ does it for you. All you have to do is to refuse to give in to the old impulse. Jesus will take care of the rest."

Other workers were making discoveries about themselves. Patti, the brunette from Kansas, had been praying that God would show her what to do. One afternoon in late winter she came into my office with two little black boys who wore only rags to protect them against the snow and chill wind outside.

"This is Juan—and Pete," she said, pushing the boys toward my desk. "They were in the grocery store hoping to steal some food. I think God wants us to clean out our basement so the little kids in the neighborhood can have a place to hear about Jesus."

Our basement had an outside street entrance. There was a large front room full of junk, and we had prayed that God would show us what to do with that room. We had also prayed about a way to reach the little ones on the streets, and I had thought God would send us a children's worker.

"Who is going to tell these kids about Jesus?" I looked at Patti and she blushed slightly.

"I've been praying about them a lot lately," she said. "It seems I just can't get these kids off my mind. I told God I'd work with them if He'd teach me how. I thought maybe we could start Kids' Crusades and have story hours every day. We could invite the parents and the older brothers and sisters to come to our family-night chapel service—" She was talking eagerly, and Pete and Juan stood nodding, eyes bright and alert, looking from Patti to me and back again.

"We'll need some plywood and paint to fix up that room—" I didn't get any further; Patti grabbed Juan and

Pete, hugged them, and exclaimed, "Praise God! Did you hear that, boys? Now you just watch and see how God gets us the material to fix up that room—and someone to do the work. We'll have a story hour next week!"

Amazing, I thought. *Patti, the quiet one who found it so difficult to tell adults about Jesus.* God had certainly picked the right job for her!

Then there was Danny. From the gutters in Brooklyn to jail and then to Teen Challenge. He'd become like a little brother to us, and for several months we watched him fight his own inward battle.

One day he came to our apartment. Ona served coffee and pie and we talked.

"I'm scared," Danny confessed. "I know I'm going to have to go to school; the thought keeps hounding me day and night. I don't think I have what it takes."

"That's good, Danny," I said. "That way you'll have to trust God in everything."

Danny went to Wisconsin to enroll in Bible college. After the first semester he sent us the results—straight A's in every subject!

It seemed incredible. For some time Ona and I had prayed that God would add an evangelist to our team—someone who could travel around the country, appear before high school assemblies and college groups, talk in churches and at rallies. We were receiving a steady stream of invitations to send speakers—and increasingly we were asked to talk before large congregations in suburban churches. The large "middle America" of suburbia, the sophisticated, well-informed, affluent society was feeling the rebellion of a generation of truth-seekers ready to explode the double standards of their parents and plunge themselves into the phony euphoria of drugs and sex.

These people didn't want pat answers or religious, pious double-talk. They needed to hear the truth, told by someone who had lived both the counterfeit and the real. And they needed to hear it in words they could accept and understand. The thought seemed farfetched, but I could already envision Danny in the pulpit.

VIII

THE summer season was well under way when Richard arrived from Maine. He called from the bus station and I sent some summer workers who knew him from Bible college to pick him up. They came back with the van piled high with expensive-looking luggage and told me that Richard had left the pile of suitcases in the middle of the great transit hall to wait for them at the entrance.

"It's a good thing God sends guardian angels to look after His little ones." Harold shook his head. "No one goes off and leaves good-looking stuff sitting in a bus depot without having it stolen."

Richard looked a little upset. He explained that he had never been to a big city before, having grown up with his grandparents in a small village in Maine where everybody knows everybody and no one steals another's luggage.

I asked Harold if anybody had explained to Richard that our unmarried male workers have to sleep in the men's dorm with the new converts and that each has only a minimal space for clothes and personal belongings. Harold shook his head.

There was a bright smile on Richard's face as he said, "I didn't think there'd be much room, so I brought only a few clothes."

I looked at the stack of suitcases and thought that there were probably enough clothes in them to outfit the entire dorm. If Richard thought this was a luxury summer resort, he was in for a rude awakening. I bit my tongue to keep from making a sharp comment. Richard would have to learn the hard way, like the rest of us, and I hoped he was made of the kind of stuff that could take it.

I watched the fellows carry the suitcases upstairs and sat down behind my desk with a sigh of exasperation. Richard was convinced God had called him to Teen Challenge; yet I felt certain that I couldn't send him out on the streets with the other summer workers. They often met rough characters and had to stand up to mockery and verbal abuse, sometimes even rocks and fists. What could I do with Richard?

Half-an-hour later he was back in my office. He looked a bit pale, but resolute when he said, "Okay, put me to work."

On an impulse I said, "You're our new choir director. Go see what you can do."

"Who's in the choir?" Richard sounded enthusiastic.

"No one, yet," I apologized. "You go start one. You can recruit workers and addicts—anyone in the building who's got a voice. The piano is in the chapel." *That should keep him busy for some time,* I thought.

When Richard had left, Harold popped in the door. "Have you seen Richard yet?" he asked.

"Sure, he's gone to start a choir. Why?" Apparently I'd missed something.

"Didn't he tell you?" Harold looked a little embarrassed, and I shook my head.

"No—tell me what?"

"Some of the workers in the dorm decided to play a joke on Richard. One of them pretended to jump him with a knife." I wasn't surprised that someone had tried to take advantage of him.

I could feel a slow anger grow inside. "Have you guys lost your senses? Were any of the converts there to see it?"

Harold shook his head. "No, they were all gone on a work detail. The fellow who did it pretended to be an addict. He didn't mean any harm . . ."

"And Richard—how did he take it?" That was what I had to know.

"A couple of the other guys pretended to hold the fellow with the knife, and Richard just stood there, quiet-like, looking straight at them without flinching. At last he said, 'The Lord brought me here; I guess He can take care of me too!' Then he turned and walked right out the door. I figured he was on his way to tell you."

I pounded my fist on the desk. "Look," I said. "You go tell those guys to get on their knees before the Lord—and then to ask Richard's forgiveness. Another stupid trick like that and whoever is responsible goes out the door."

Harold ducked out, and I began to pace the floor. It looked as if I had a problem on my hands. Richard was going to be a favorite sitting duck for pranks; there was always one in every crowd. How well I remembered others like him! We used to call them "sissy" or "teacher's pet" or "mommy's boy," and for some unexplainable reason the rest of us found endless entertainment in short-sheeting them in the dorm or sending them on meaningless errands to the dean's office. Richard seemed a natural. He was gentle, well-mannered, and—I feared—gullible.

How would he be able to get along with the converts? Would they spot him as a "softie" and take advantage of him? It seems that each one of our workers has to go through a period of personal testing by our converts. Only when they have proved themselves firm in their attitudes do the converts respond with respect. For some of our new workers this is a difficult time, and some give up and leave us. For those who stick with it, the testing proves to be a time of personal growth, and they emerge stronger in faith, trusting God, and sure of themselves in a new way.

I honestly feared that Richard didn't have what it would take.

"God help him," I prayed out loud. "He's Your child, Lord; now make him a man."

I opened the door to the hallway. Strains of music were drifting down from the chapel. I'd never heard music quite like that around Teen Challenge before. Voices blended in perfect harmony, singing the chorus to "How Great Thou Art" with a background of piano music in such exuberant tones that I thought Richard must have brought a tape recording of a choir back at school. If he could just make our kids sound half that good we'd go spread the gospel in song all over town!

The music stopped, and I heard Richard's voice. "Okay, let's do it once more, and this time, Sunday, you do the solo."

The mellow tones from the trumpet filled the building, and I didn't wait any longer but ran up the stairs two steps at a time.

THE SOUL PATROL

In the chapel door I stopped short. Richard was at the piano, handling the keyboard as if it was an extension of his hands. The music came rippling out like water in a spring brook. Sunday had lowered her trumpet and joined the rest of the group who were lined up facing Richard, their eyes watching intently for his signal. Then, without missing a note on the piano, Richard nodded for them to begin.

I sat down in the back of the chapel. I'd never seen anyone in such complete command of a group of singers, directing them simply with a nod or a look. I had worried about the ex-addicts not respecting Richard. Here he was obviously the master of the situation. In a short hour he had taken a group of young people who had never sung together before—some of them had never been in a choir—some of them were fresh from the back alleys of the ghetto—and they sounded professional. I was thrilled—and I was learning . . .

Listening to the beginnings of our "choir," I began to realize that God had intended music to mean something special at our center, more than just release and rejoicing and praise during our worship service. Here was a way, a wonderful new way, for ex-addicts and workers alike to learn the self-discipline of training their voices to blend in harmony with others.

One problem most drug addicts share is that of loneliness and isolation. What drove most of them into drugs or alcohol or sex was a breakdown in real communication with their surroundings, an inability to relate in love, to reach out and touch another human being and be accepted and understood.

The drug addict, the alcoholic, and the prostitute are usually miserably lonely beings, in spite of the fact that they may "run in packs." I've watched them in a shooting gallery or in a bar—together in a group, yet each one lost in his own reverie or dreams, without any real concern for anyone else.

One of the necessary steps towards rehabilitation or healing is learning to relate to others, learning to be part of a group in a meaningful way. Jesus puts it bluntly: "Love one another. Love your neighbor as yourself." Maybe the hardest thing for anyone is to learn to love himself. Getting to know who he is and what he is. It's a little bit like finding out where he belongs in a choir—with the sopranos, altos or tenors.

A turning point in the life of an ex-addict comes when he begins to believe that Jesus Christ not only loves him, but needs him. Each has been given special talents. He may have hidden his talent and never known it was there. Nevertheless, God planted it there for His use, and nobody else in the whole world can be or do what God intended that one individual to be and do. In God's Kingdom everyone counts.

I've watched the change come over converts—and staff workers—as they've discovered who they really are and what their talents are. Paul talks much about that in his letter to the Corinthians—about the different gifts and abilities, how they are equally important, and how they make up the body of Christ—all of them together.

And no one is happy in the wrong slot.

Richard was obviously in the right slot, at least as far as the music was concerned. Now all he'd have to do was prove himself a man in the streets. If he didn't have the backbone for the rougher aspects of our work, he'd have to go—in spite of his musical talents. All of the rest of us have found that our talents and abilities have to be subject to God's discipline and control before we can really be trusted with the job.

There was Candy over in the soprano section, skinny and

pale and not looking too enthusiastic about the situation, but she was there. And she was singing, which in itself was a bit of a miracle.

Candy had been at the center a little over three weeks. She'd been released into our custody from the court, and it was obvious that she was with us just because jail would be worse. Ona had counseled with her, and had come away shaking her head. I had come home to find my wife on her knees by the bed, crying and praying for Candy. From the looks of her red, tear-swollen eyes I knew she'd been at it for hours.

We both knew that if Candy didn't change for the better soon, we would have to send her away. She was sullen, sarcastic, and often downright cruel. When she first came to the center we had explained that in order to stay, she would have to commit herself to our program. Candy was only seventeen, but she had been on dope for five years and had spent time in jail and in mental hospitals.

Candy came from the suburbs of a large southern city where her father was a well-to-do engineer and her mother a bridge-playing, cocktail-drinking socialite. Candy had always been well ahead of her class in school; in fact, she was something of a whiz kid and had early gotten into trouble because of her know-it-all attitude toward teachers.

I'm sure it didn't take her long to size up the situation at Teen Challenge. Apparently she decided the easiest way out would be to put on the appearance of what she considered to be a Christian and stick it out with us rather than go back to a jail cell or a hospital where she soon would get tired of playing cat and mouse with the psychiatrists. (Candy, of course, would be considering herself in the role of cat.)

We've had other kids like Candy. They've put on a good

show, but you can't fake a relationship with Christ. Jesus said you can know a tree by its fruits. So it is with being a Christian. It isn't what you say, but what you are.

Candy learned the language of a convert quicker than most. She observed the others in chapel and came to the altar for prayer with a good show of tears, the accompanying bright smile, and "Thank you, Jesus, for saving my soul." She carried a Bible around and talked a great deal about how "groovy" Jesus is, but Candy obviously didn't know what or whom she was talking about. Her large gray eyes remained dull and hostile; her smile was forced; and she moved restlessly from room to room, talking aimlessly and endlessly about things of the past.

One of our rules at Teen Challenge is that our converts do not talk about their former life with drugs. We've found that dwelling on past experiences only causes our converts to revert to depression and temptation. The most difficult part of their rehabilitation is to train their minds to new ways of thinking. Talking about the past can be a stumbling block for many. Even in our counseling sessions, we spend very little time discussing the whys and wherefores of drug addiction. As Christians we believe that Jesus came to forgive our sins and make all things new. God casts our sins into the sea of forgetfulness and puts up a sign—it says "No Fishing." Our job is to put our minds on Christ, on our present life in Him, and hope for the future.

For Candy it seemed impossible to stop looking at the past. She was a real problem in the girls' dorm. Sunday was supervisor of girls, and Candy had a way of stirring them up, confiding to one what another had said, and then going back to the first one to say, "and you should hear what she thinks of you!"

The only reason we could keep Candy was that she was the youngest one in the dorm, and the others were stable enough to withstand her attacks. It was clear that if a new girl should come, she would need all our attention, and Candy would be too much of a risk.

Yet we thanked God that it was possible for Candy to stay. Ona was deeply moved by Candy's plight; the girl had obviously been so deeply hurt that she was completely unable to let down her guard and trust anyone.

Slowly Ona got much of the story.

When she was twelve, Candy discovered by accident that she was adopted. It had been one of those cruel incidents, where her mother, under the influence of alcohol, had turned and said, "You'll be nothing but a slut—just like your *real* mother!"

Candy turned for solace to a group of kids in her school who turned her on to pot, sex, mescaline, and LSD. She became the "doll" of a motorcycle gang at the age of fourteen. During one of their dope parties, another girl overdosed and died in the bedroom. Candy watched her and pleaded with the fellows to get help. One of them looked at her and said, "You want to get us all busted?" Considering the situation, Candy agreed that would be too risky. When the girl was dead, they put her in the trunk of a car and took her to the apartment house where she had lived with her thrice-divorced mother. They put the body on the doorstep, rang the bell, and took off.

From then on Candy developed a keen interest in animals, and always pleaded with her boyfriend to stop his cycle whenever a turtle crossed the road or if they spotted a wounded cat or dog. Tenderly, Candy would nurse the animal back to life.

After the experience with the girl overdosing, Candy had several bad trips on LSD and was forced to change to speed, then to coke and heroin. Then one day the guys were racing on an open stretch of road outside of town. A small dog got in the way, and Candy's friend killed it. That night the gang had planned a big dope party. Candy waited till everyone had turned on, then sneaked out and called the police who raided the place and put everyone in jail—everyone except Candy, that is. As soon as the fellows were out on bail they looked her up, took her to an abandoned shack by the river, and held her while her ex-boyfriend stuck the needle in her vein and shot her up with speed. They knew that she was on heroin, and the combination had the effect they wanted—it nearly drove her out of her mind. When she was "high" enough, the boys took turns raping her. She stayed in the shack for three days—unable to move or think. Then she went home, gathered some of her things and hitchhiked to Chicago where she soon found friends among a far-left hippie-colony. She stayed long enough to help put out a couple of underground newspapers; then, in a fit of homesickness, she called her parents and said she wanted to come home. They told her they loved her and had forgiven all and sent an airplane ticket. For the first time in several years Candy felt a tinge of hope.

Her parents did not show up at the airport, but an ambulance was waiting to take Candy to a nearby hospital where her parents were ready to check her into the psychiatric ward. After six months she was released with a clean bill of health by the psychiatrist who noted that her intelligence was near genius, but that she was emotionally strung out and somehow wrongly motivated.

Candy threw herself back into the life she knew best, and now she was highly motivated by a consuming hatred for her parents, the police, and all authority, including the motorcycle gangs. She set about to make herself kingpin among the pushers and managed to organize several flower festivals, love-ins and peace demonstrations—all of them designed to end in riots, headaches for the police, and a dope-peddler's heaven for Candy.

From then on, it was in and out of jail, always slipping out from under the charges, until she got caught on one of her trips to the north. This time, she had stopped for a party in Philadelphia. All went well until she saw a young couple give their baby LSD. It was meant to be the highlight of the party, watching the baby "trip." Candy watched the infant kick and toss helplessly, and suddenly got nauseated. He looked too much like the puppy dog her boyfriend had run over. She left the party, called the police, then went back to keep an eye on the baby. She was there when the narcotics agents closed in, and for the first time in her life she pleaded guilty to the charge of possession of narcotics.

The way she told it to Ona, she would rather be busted and put in jail by the police than be caught again by the dopers she had "narked" on.

"You straight people have your kind of justice," she told Ona during their first interview. "We've got ours. Your side puts people safely behind bars. We kill. I'd rather be caught by you."

Candy was a loner, and our hearts ached for her. If another girl tried to put an arm around her, Candy shrank back as if she was afraid of being touched.

We had prayed for a way to reach her, some way to involve her in the group, some way to make her feel part of our Teen Challenge family.

Now she was singing with the rest of them—Richard had obviously not taken her usual "no" for an answer. I could hear her voice among the others, clear, with the rich quality of a potential soloist. There was a slight blush on her cheeks. Perhaps God was working another miracle—and as usual, His way was much better than anything we could have planned.

IX

I MISSED Danny more than I had thought I would. He had traveled with me on speaking tours across the country and, in his quiet way, had been a wonderful companion and partner. When he gave his testimony, young people stopped to listen. Danny was quiet almost to the point of being shy, but he spoke with a sincerity and authority that carried a great deal of weight. Danny was for real.

His letters from school were enthusiastic, and we were happy for him. Still, Ona and I were beginning to count the months till he would be with us again. The demands on me for speaking engagements were more than I could handle alone.

Our music ministry was rapidly becoming an important part of our evangelistic outreach; wherever our choir or one of our trios or quartets sang, we would get immediate invitations to come back. Still, we desperately needed someone like Danny.

There seemed no apparent reason for concern, yet I was feeling a growing uneasiness about him. Whenever we talked about our plans at the center involving him, I'd get a strange feeling of unreality.

At last I confided in Ona and we prayed about it. She, too, had felt uneasy about something, but it was the kind of vague feeling you can't put your finger on. It just stays there. We prayed that God would keep Danny safe, and that He would bring him back to us—if that was His perfect will. With a slight twinge I also prayed, "God, if it is Your will to use him somewhere else, let that be."

Shortly afterward we got a letter from Danny mentioning a girl named Judi. Danny had never been one for dating much—his shyness alone kept him from talking to girls. Now he spoke with great enthusiasm of Judi, who was a music major at the college and played the piano when Danny's trio sang.

"That's it!" Ona said when I shared the letter with her. "That explains the feelings we've been having. Danny is in love and wants to get married. Maybe the girl doesn't like the idea of Teen Challenge."

The wedding was in June, and Judi was adorable. It was obvious that the two of them were very much in love, and Danny spoke vaguely of the future. Probably he would stay in school for another two years; of course they both wanted to serve the Lord.

Ona and I returned to Philadelphia, reassured that Danny had married just the girl for him, but not at all sure of where that left Teen Challenge. Judi was sweet and kind, well-groomed and quite accomplished in music—the perfect minister's wife. She had been raised in the church by devoted parents. Her father had a secure job with the government, and Judi had been taught that security and a savings account were practically synonymous. Could she make the switch to house-keeping on faith? Giving all to God and expecting Him to sup-ply all needs?

Danny and Judi spent three weeks at the center during the summer. Danny worked on the streets, and Judi helped out in the office. Somehow, they didn't seem to give their all to the work. Summer is a busy season, and I didn't have much time to talk to them. When we did sit down together, the conversation was strained. They left for Minnesota and fall term at the college, and I knew that Danny really didn't want to come back to us. He hadn't said it, I just knew. Again we renewed our prayers, asking that God's will be done, and for quite a while we heard very little from Danny and Judi. Their notes were brief and friendly, that was all.

Then one day I received a phone call from Danny. There was a new intensity to his voice: "Bob," he said, "God has been calling us to Teen Challenge. We've fought it, but it's for real. We're coming back."

"What about Judi?" I remembered Dave Wilkerson, who told us that God always calls both husband and wife.

"I told her before we were married that I wouldn't go back to Teen Challenge, but she was always afraid I would change my mind. Then she saw your movie and cried all the way through. God has called her too."

Judi and Danny moved into the apartment next to the girls' dorm. The biggest problem was having to share the bath-room with the girls. I could sympathize—that's how we had lived in New York. Judi worked in the office and took on the job as organist in our music department. We'd bought a beau-tiful organ with money we received from our first record, and it was clear from the start that Judi and Richard had our music department well in hand.

I thought all was working out smoothly, but it soon became apparent that Danny was worried.

I asked him one day, "Is it financial, Danny? Anything I can do to help?"

Danny shook his head. "It's Judi," he said. "It's hard for her to understand why we're so strict around here." He looked at me. "Frankly, she's a little afraid of you," he said. "You said something about short dresses one day, and she's always afraid hers isn't long enough."

I wanted to laugh, but this was no laughing matter. Discipline was an essential ingredient in our program. Our workers couldn't handle the disciplining of addicts until they themselves had learned self-discipline. First of all they had to see the need for discipline.

Judi had been raised in the sheltered surroundings of a church family and a Bible college where certain rules and regulations were followed almost automatically. There had been no need for rigid enforcement there. But there *was* such a need at Teen Challenge. I often think that our workers are like soldiers on the front lines. The enemy is right there, and one little slipup can mean death. Don't light a match; don't make a noise; don't go blundering off somewhere, forgetting your weapon. Stay alert.

The situation is completely different in an army camp back home. The discipline slacks off; if you can cheat on inspection or steal a quick smoke while you're on guard duty—so what? Nobody gets hurt, you figure.

Kids who are raised in churches can get that way too. Parents force them to attend Sunday School and church; maybe religion was crammed down their throats. Perhaps they joined the church just because the youth group was a lot of fun.

Judi had grown up with kids like that, the kind who sit on the back pew and pass notes during the sermon. When she first came to Teen Challenge, our way of doing things seemed pretty far-out. Yet it was important that she come to see that it had to be that way.

Judi is a very pretty girl, and her clothes were of the latest style. It is true that our girls have to wear their dresses longer than most young women on the outside. This isn't because we are old fogies. It's just that short skirts can prove too much of a distraction for some of our converts who were hung up on sex as well as dope. Girl addicts who come in have to get rid of all makeup and clothes that are too suggestive. Slacks and shorts are forbidden too.

So Judi's hems had to go down, something she was obviously unhappy about.

"I'm sorry," I said to Danny. "But Judi will have to learn, or her attitude will hurt the other girls. They don't particularly like wearing long skirts either."

"If we could just live away from the center," Danny said. "I think it would be easier if Judi could sort of relax at home."

"Let's pray about it," I suggested. "But I think God will keep you two here till Judi fully understands why our rules have to be."

Danny nodded. "I know," he said. "It's Judi's hurdle, and she'll make it and praise the Lord for it too!" He grinned. "I bet the Lord has an apartment waiting for us right now; all we have to do is grow into it!"

I laughed with him, sure I knew what he was talking about. It seemed all of us were having to grow up into what

God wanted to give us next. And some of us were having growing pains.

Karen was our new supervisor of girls, and at first I didn't
think she could handle the job. She was small with dark hair
framing a thin face dominated by large gray eyes. She looked
like a little girl, and when she first arrived she confessed to
Ona that she was really scared to death. "I was born with a
natural yellow streak; I'm just a coward," she said. She had
come wanting to do evangelistic street work, but that first summer she was part of a trio and did as little work with the addicts as possible.

"I just don't know how to handle them," she said.

Yet Ona felt strongly that Karen should be supervisor of
girls. "I know the Lord has given her a talent for working with
the girls," she insisted.

Karen agreed to join Ona in prayer about it, and after several hours of prayer and meditation in the chapel she emerged
red-eyed but determined. "I guess God knows I'm so weak in
myself that I'm going to have to rely on Him," she said. "He'll
have to teach me all about it."

Karen wasn't just talking. She meant business. She spent
hours on her knees asking God to strengthen her ability to love
the girls, to understand their needs, and to be firm when
firmness was needed.

The results began to show up. The girls didn't like it; they
had been getting away with temper tantrums and shirking of
duties before. Not any longer.

"I'm scared to death when one of them says 'I don't want
to,'" Karen confided in Ona. "But God has shown me that if

I am protective and indulgent, those girls will have to suffer later."

Karen's first hurdle came with Kathy. We knew it wouldn't be easy to handle; yet I felt that God had somehow arranged to bring Kathy and Karen together in that particular situation. They needed each other.

Kathy and Karen had been roommates in Bible college. When I came to the campus for a rally, Kathy came to see me. I could tell she had problems, although she tried to pretend that everything was fine and that she only wanted information about working for Teen Challenge.

I gathered that she had been a recent convert and had come to Bible school against her parents' will. Now she said she wanted to work in Philadelphia. I watched her dark brown eyes dart restlessly around the room while we were talking. She was wearing far too much makeup, her skirts were too short, and heavy earrings jangled whenever she moved her head. Kathy was not a likely candidate for a Teen Challenge staff worker. Yet something told me she needed to come to us for help.

I suggested she come for a visit to see how things were at the center. "Then you can decide for yourself," I said. "Come anytime."

One day I got a long-distance phone call from Kathy.

"I'm coming tomorrow," she said brightly. "The plane gets to Philadelphia at three. I'll call you from the airport."

The next day at three o'clock, Sunday was at the airport, dressed in a yellow suit and walking a gray poodle. When Kathy called, it was to say that she didn't want to come to the center after all. We told her to wait at the airport and to talk to Sunday, at least. As we described the yellow suit and gray poodle, Kathy gasped at the other end of the line.

"She's standing outside the phone booth!" she said. There was no escaping; Sunday seemed to know who Kathy was and brought her to the center to stay "at least for a while." We found out later that she had come on the plane quite "by accident." After telling me she was coming, she had chickened out, gone to a local dance hall, and spent the entire thirty-five dollars she needed for the plane fare. The next morning she was dismayed to see two of her girl friends come to her apartment and offer to take her to the airport. She was ashamed to admit what she'd done, and packed her two suitcases, thinking she could somehow get away from her friends at the airport. In the car one of the girls handed her an envelope and said: "Just a little something God told us you'd be needing." With shaking hands Kathy opened the envelope. It contained thirty-five dollars!

Kathy's hang-up wasn't dope—it was sex and guys. In fact, any fellow was like a magnet to her, and the feeling was often mutual. Kathy was cute and cuddly, with large brown eyes and a teasing smile. When she walked across the room, boys just naturally stopped and stared. Obviously, Kathy could get herself and others into trouble quite easily.

Ona explained the rules, and Kathy sulked a bit, but agreed to wash off all makeup, remove the earrings, and try to walk across a room without moving her body quite so suggestively.

Things appeared to be going smoothly, but one afternoon a week or so after she arrived, Kathy was gone. Somebody said she had gone out the back door. Sunday and Peg ran down the alley after her. Around the corner they found her—snuggled tightly up to Toni, a Puerto Rican convert who had been at our center for nearly three months.

Toni ran when he saw the two girls coming, but Kathy smiled brightly, smoothed her long black hair, and said, "It's such a beautiful day, I thought it would be nice to take a walk."

Sunday and Peg marched her back to the center and into my office where Kathy hung her head and said she was sorry.

"I really didn't mean any harm, Brother Bartlett," she said. I told her that we ordinarily send girls home if they are found with one of our boys, but I would make an exception if she would promise to pray about the problem until God could make her really see the danger of her ways.

"You know you don't really mean it when you say you're sorry," I said, and Kathy blushed. "You're just sorry you got caught, isn't that true?" Kathy nodded.

"As long as you feel that way it will happen again and again," I continued. "One day you'll really get hurt."

It soon became obvious that Kathy had already been hurt. I'd watched her pick at her food, and Karen reported that she was often sick at her stomach.

"I think she needs to see a doctor," Karen told Ona.

A Christian obstetrician takes care of our young women without charge. He took one look at Kathy and said, "You're going to have a baby."

Amid a flood of tears Kathy confessed that she had been seeing a boy at school regularly during her last semester.

"I knew it was wrong," she sobbed. "I just couldn't quit."

The next few months were hard ones for Kathy—and for Karen, who became directly responsible for Kathy's daily care and discipline. There would be a temper tantrum—over something as simple as taking vitamin pills. Kathy would refuse to eat the proper foods, and patiently, Karen would force her to swallow every bite. Kathy was bigger than Karen, and I've seen Karen standing with feet apart and hands planted firmly on her hips watching Kathy stomp up and down on the floor, yelling, "You're no better than I am; you've got no right to tell me what to do!"

"Okay." Karen's voice would be quiet and very firm. "Maybe *I* don't have the right to tell you—but God does. So let's both get on our knees and stay there till He can tell us what to do."

Still fuming and fussing, Kathy would get to her knees, and the two girls knelt side by side in prayer. One of us would come into the chapel to find them there, tears flowing and arms around each other.

We watched the change come over both of them. Kathy softened, and as the weeks grew into months she spent an increasing number of hours on her knees in the chapel, not only in prayer for herself, but as intercessor for converts and workers with special problems. She was becoming a prayer-warrior, and often had insights into the hidden hurts of others at the center.

Karen grew stronger, and I don't know which one of the two suffered the hardest growing pains. Often Karen would unburden herself to Ona. "I can't stand being so strict," she'd say. "I know the girls hate me sometimes and call me a witch. But it's like we've got to keep the outward standards like brick walls around them while God establishes their inner stability. We get behind them and push, and they know we won't let them fall."

Judi found it hard to accept Karen's rigid disciplining of the girls. Some of the converts took advantage of the situation and came to Judi to find sympathy when Karen had been extra-strict.

One girl was in constant trouble. She was Tammy, a fifteen-year-old black girl who had come to us with a hang-up on dope and boys. Whenever we turned our backs, Tammy would manage to exchange words with one of the fellows. When caught, she could respond with filthy language and screaming fits. Karen was having a hard time controlling her.

Encouraged by Candy, who was well aware of the situation, Tammy would run to Judi and tell her how unfair Karen had been. The result was predictable: Tammy was getting the attention she wanted and remained as uncontrollable as ever while tension mounted between Judi and Karen.

Hidden resentment and tension between any of us at Teen Challenge is like poison in the soup or sugar in the gasoline tank. The whole center suffers.

We're not like other organizations where things can go on functioning even if some of the workers are no longer on speaking terms.

We're not an organization, we're an organism, and our life blood is the Holy Spirit. Resentments or grudges block the power and the presence of the Holy Spirit. Our work slows down and comes to a grinding halt. There's nothing to do then but to stop and pray until the trouble is uncovered and healed.

Karen and Judi apologized to one another whenever there had been an overt disagreement, but something was obviously still smoldering under the surface.

"Tammy is really a very sensitive child who needs much

love and understanding," Judi would say; and Karen would retort, "Unless she learns to control herself, she'll never grow up."

Then one afternoon Tammy was in the kitchen goofing off instead of helping with the dishes. Karen told her to get busy; and instead of doing as she was told, Tammy picked up a sharp butcher knife, pointed it at Karen, and began backing toward the back door.

"I'm tired of being bossed around," she said. "I'm going out to have some fun."

"Give me the knife." Karen spoke firmly, holding out her hand, and Tammy laughed.

"You don't have any right to tell me what to do," she said. "Who do you think you are?"

The door to the dining room was open, and Judi walked by. She stopped and gasped when she saw what was happening. "Tammy!" she cried out. "Put down that knife!"

Tammy seemed to enjoy the scene and shouted back at Judi, "Don't try to stop me—I'm not gonna hurt anybody—I just want to go out and have some fun."

At this point, Tom, our prison chaplain, walked in the back door, took one look at the scene, and stepped up to Tammy. Firmly, he took the knife out of her hand and put it in the open drawer; then, grasping Tammy around the middle, he turned her over his knee and planted several firm pats on her rear.

Back on her feet, cocksure Tammy had been reduced to a tearful and subdued little girl.

"Next time I'll use the paddle," Tom warned. "Now go do the dishes!"

Judi looked at Karen and held out her hand.

"Please," she said, "will you help me pray? I think God is telling me I need to learn something about discipline."

Karen smiled. "Me too," she said. "God's been telling me for weeks I haven't got enough authority."

X

DANNY and Judi stood in the center of my office, holding hands and looking as if they had just seen a vision.

Danny stared at me intently. "Would you mind repeating what you just said? I don't think I heard you right."

"It's very simple," I said. "I want to apologize to you, because while you were touring Wisconsin, a new couple arrived to work at the center, and we had no place to put them except your apartment. Now we've got this run-down house over in Kensington that a church would let us use rent-free. Maybe you'd like to fix it up and live there."

Danny and Judi looked as if they were ready to burst, and I hurriedly added, "Of course, I'm sure the other couple won't mind giving you back your old apartment, if you'd rather."

"Praise the Lord! Thank you, Jesus!" Judi threw her arms up in the air and twirled around on the floor. Danny grinned from ear to ear.

"We've been praying about getting a place of our own," he

said. "We asked God to provide the place and the circumstances. Looks like He's done it."

"I'll be gone to Israel for the next week or so," I said. "You make your own decision."

I watched them go. They looked so happy, like two children about to receive a wonderful treat. I knew what the place in Kensington was like. The other brownstones on the block didn't look too bad; their owners had fixed them up pretty nice. But the street was a hangout for motorcycle gangs and rowdy teen-agers, and our building looked as if it ought to be condemned. I sighed. It seemed that was the way God preferred to do things—show us that He could take the things we despised and rejected and make something out of them.

"Lord," I prayed aloud, "when are You going to find us a house for the girls? I don't care what kind, Lord, just as long as it is the one You've picked for us."

I had to laugh to myself. Things had changed over the last few years, and I had changed. Sure, I was still tempted to dictate to God once in a while. And of course that invariably led to a deflating experience when I ran ahead of Him into a firmly closed door.

"Lord," I said into the emptiness of my office, "Lord . . ." And suddenly I felt a slow tingling of my spine as I realized that my office was far from empty. Jesus said, "I am with you always," and He wasn't just talking.

"Help me, Jesus," I said. "You've brought us a long way; You've opened those other three centers for us and staffed them; You've helped us make a movie; and through us You are touching hundreds of young people in this city and across the nation. Now You're even taking me to Israel, and maybe someday we'll have a center for evangelistic outreach there.

Please, Jesus, You know I get bigheaded sometimes. Please don't let me run ahead of You. Please pull the rug from under me if I do . . ."

The air in my office seemed filled with a warmth and light, and I leaned my head against the back of my chair. The stack of papers on my desk, the pending gasoline bill, the girls who'd been harassed in Rittenhouse Square—without realizing it, I had allowed tension to creep in. Slowly the peace flowed through me. I felt my shoulders sag a little and the muscles in my arms and legs relax.

"Sorry, Jesus," I said to the light and warmth around me. "Tension is lack of trust. I guess I thought I had to carry the burden on my own shoulders again. Here, You can have it! And thank You for Your peace."

When the doorbell rang I got to my feet. It was nearly midnight. Outside stood a stocky middle-aged man, well-dressed, but in obvious anguish. A long haired teen-ager dressed in dirty jeans and a grease-stained buckskin jacket slouched against the wall. The sallow skin color and the blank, indifferent, stare told the story without words.

"I called—you said you'd talk to my son . . ." The man shifted his weight nervously from one foot to the other. I thought of the endless trail he must have followed, from doctor to counselor to social worker to police station . . . "Please help my son—"

"Come in!" I held the door wide open and pointed toward my office.

The man sank down into a comfortable chair with a deep sigh of relief, but the boy remained standing near the door. His eyes had quickly taken in his surroundings—the two windows

—how do you open them? He had watched me lock and bolt the inside of the front door. It had made him obviously uneasy.

"This is Ricky." The man spoke eagerly, hopefully, and the youth stared at me silently. The hostility hung like a heavy freeze between us.

"Hi, Ricky!"

There was no response, and the father interrupted anxiously. "Ricky doesn't talk much; he's been through a lot lately. We've been trying to get help, and he's spent several months in mental hospitals and in jail."

I looked at Ricky. "Do you want help?" He shrugged, and the father said, "Sure he does."

"Why did you come here tonight, Ricky?" I watched him shrug again and cast a quick glance at his father.

"I guess maybe I want to find out about your program." He dug in his pocket and came up with a crumpled package of cigarettes. "Mind if I smoke?" He didn't wait for an answer but stuck the cigarette in his mouth.

"Sorry, Ricky, no smoking." I said it matter-of-factly and he laughed.

"Come on, preacher, I'm not stuck in here yet; I need a smoke!"

"Sorry, Ricky, those are firm rules." His hands shook when he put the cigarette back into the package.

"Okay," he said. "What's the beef about this place? I want to get out of here."

His father sat slumped over in the chair; his brown eyes were brimming with tears, and he coughed suddenly and dug for a handkerchief to blow his nose.

"What do you know about Jesus?" I asked quietly.

"He's a gilded statue in a church, so what?"

"No, Ricky." I shook my head. "He's alive; He can take away your hang-ups and set you free; and He can fill that empty place inside you." Ricky wasn't paying much attention to me. *God,* I thought, *only Your Holy Spirit can get inside that head of his and show him what it's all about.*

"This center is full of fellows like you who've been dope addicts for years. They turned to Jesus and He helped them. Some of them have been clean for months; some of them have gone on from here to college or jobs on the outside. They're free because Jesus Christ lives in them."

I searched Ricky's eyes for a glimmer of light and found none.

"It's strictly voluntary," I said. "God created you with a free will; it's your choice. If you decide to come in with us it will be tough, because you've got to break the old habits. No smoking, no talking to girls, no liberty. Your family can visit you here and attend our open family-night chapel services every Tuesday. We keep a rigid schedule. You'll have duties to perform. We get up, eat, work, play—all on a schedule. We have lots of sports to build up your health again; we go to church nearly every night; and we spend much time in Bible study and prayer."

I saw no response of interest in Ricky's eyes, but I continued talking. Somehow I couldn't get rid of my inner vision of Danny in the jail cell in Brooklyn.

"The difference between Teen Challenge and some other rehabilitation centers is that we don't expect you to pull through alone. We know that God is real, that He is a supernatural power who can come into us through Jesus Christ and the Holy Spirit. The addicts who come here go through withdrawal without medication, and every one of them experiences something of the power of God coming into him to ease the pain and bring him through—as much as they let Him."

"No medication? No doctor?" There was a flicker of something deep in Ricky's eyes. "You guys ever get in trouble with the law—somebody dyin' on you or somethin'?"

I smiled. "We've got a doctor on twenty-four-hour call, Ricky," I said. "Everybody who comes here gets a complete physical. Besides, you kick cold turkey in jail, don't you?" He nodded. "And like I said about God, He never lets anybody down when they trust in Him. The addicts who kick here do it a lot easier than they've ever done it before; some of them don't have any pain at all."

Ricky shook his head. "Naw," he said, "I don't need no hang-up on religion. I'm a free man now, and I don't hurt no place. Maybe sometime I'll consider it." He straightened up and looked at his father.

"C'mon, Dad. I did like I promised. I listened to the preacher. Now let's go."

"Ricky," I stood up to face him. "You've heard it now. You've heard that Jesus is for real; He cares about you; He needs you. We at Teen Challenge care too. I'll be praying for you. Anytime you really want to come, we'll be looking for you."

A thin smile crossed Ricky's face. "Thanks, preach, but don't waste your breath."

He walked out the door ahead of his father, cockily swaggering his hips, and the older man looked at me apologetically, trying to fight back his tears. I shook his hand.

"Maybe," I said, "when Ricky gets caught in a tight squeeze he'll see that he needs help. Nobody can decide for him."

I watched them go down the sidewalk and stop at the corner. The father appeared to be talking to his son. He put his hand on the sleeve of the buckskin jacket, and I watched Ricky shake it off. Without looking at his father, he walked off with that same cocky swagger. The father stood motionless, watching, then turned slowly on his heels and began walking the other way toward the bus stop.

I leaned my forehead against the cool windowpane and did nothing to hold back the sob that shook me.

"Oh, Jesus," I whispered. "Help me to bring these kids to Your cross and leave them there. You go with Ricky. You know how to get through to him. Thank you, Jesus."

The trip to Israel was a fantastic experience. I wanted to pinch myself, expecting to wake up on Broad Street in Philadelphia. There I was, halfway around the world from the corn-fields in Kansas, contemplating opening a combination coffeehouse, bookstore, and chapel to reach Jewish young people with the Good News about their Messiah. It was an exciting thought, the kind of way-out challenge God gives.

"You open the door, God, and I'll go through it," I promised. I didn't know when it might be, but somehow I felt certain that my dream would become a reality one day.

I'd been gone only a few days; yet it seemed as if everything had happened at the center while I was away. One way God keeps me humble—He shows me His work goes on when I'm away!

Sunday was all smiles when I asked about the gasoline bill. "Oh, that!" she said. "The day it was due we were praying in the chapel during our morning service. A white-haired man came to our door, asking for you. Danny said you were out of town and asked if someone else could help him. He shook his head, but stood there as if he didn't know what to do. Danny told him we were having chapel service, and he was welcome to join us. He did, and was in the chapel with us singing and praying during the rest of the service. Nobody knew him, and he slipped back out the door and went downstairs before anybody could speak to him. There he found Danny and handed him an envelope, said goodbye politely, and left. Danny brought the envelope to me; we opened it, and there was a check for one thousand dollars!"

How typical, I thought. *God comes through at the last minute; yet He's never too late.*

I'll never forget the Sunday afternoon just after Christmas when we held a meeting in a small church in New Jersey. The attendance hadn't been very high, and the offering was quite small. (Who can afford to give on the first Sunday after Christmas?) Yet our needs at Teen Challenge were great. We were short on money for such essentials as food and fuel and rent. January is a tough month in any budget.

After most of the people had left, a little old lady came up to me. She walked slowly and with difficulty. Her hands were red and roughened, and her coat showed the wear of many winters. She looked at me and smiled apologetically.

"Brother Bartlett," she said, "would you be staying here a little while longer this afternoon? I have some money at home I've saved for you."

We had a long way to go to get home, the roads were icy, and I was supposed to preach somewhere else that night. I was sure that the little old lady couldn't possibly have more than ten or fifteen dollars saved up. But what did Jesus say about the widows' mite?

"Sure, Ma'am," I said. "I'll be staying for a while."

I watched her walk across the frozen front lawn to a small white frame house next to the church. Every step was an effort, and I felt a sudden surge of compassion for her. The nickels and dimes she must have put aside from the grocery money— would they have gone toward a new winter coat? What joy she must have felt knowing that her pennies would help some young person find the way!

She returned carrying a brown paper bag and handed it to me with a smile that brimmed with sheer joy. I smiled back, shook her hand, and said, "God bless you, sister," then turned and left.

I didn't think to look in the paper bag until we were half-way home. Richard was with me and asked, "By the way, what did the little old lady give you?" I dug the paper bag from my pocket and handed it to him. Richard looked in the bag, then lowered his head and just sat there. I glanced at him sideways, wondering what was wrong.

"There's between two and three thousand dollars in that bag, Bob," Richard said quietly. "God took a little old lady and had her save up for years just to meet our needs at the right moment. When are we going to stop worrying about tomorrow altogether and trust Him? We keep thinking some millionaire ought to come along, and God sends a crippled little old lady . . ."

I'm beginning to learn that trusting God to meet your needs also means you don't try to anticipate His ways of doing it.

During another tight squeeze (I'm starting to think of

them as adventures: how is He going to take care of us this time?), our attorney, Harvey Steinberg, told me one day, "You know, Bob, I've been doing some research lately. You're a religious nonprofit rehabilitation center, and you really should be tax-exempt."

Right then I hadn't paid too much attention. It would be nice, but I wasn't going to get excited about it.

Harvey, a young Jew who often shook his head in amazement at our ways of doing business, had been a good friend and supporter of Teen Challenge for some time. I thought back about how I happened to meet him.

We had been praying for God to send us legal counsel. With our budget we could hardly afford to hire a lawyer. One night a young drug addict came to the center from our coffeehouse. Len was an acidhead who had been moved by the testimony of our workers. We admitted him late at night and saw him tucked in bed in the men's dorm.

A few hours later I was aroused from my sleep by a phone call. It was the police. They wanted to know if we had given Len the keys to one of our cars and permission to drive it. They were holding him for questioning at the station, since he had a record of car thefts. His attorney had been called. They asked me to come down.

Len's attorney was Harvey Steinberg, who expected his young client to be in big trouble this time.

"I don't intend to press charges," I told him. "I just want to get Len into our program and help him." Harvey Steinberg looked at me openmouthed.

"You don't want to press charges?"

I shook my head. "No, I think Len is serious this time, and I know that Jesus Christ can help him."

I explained our program of drug rehabilitation to Steinberg, who seemed much impressed when I told him of our success ratio with the addicts.

"I'm talking about your Messiah," I said, smiling, and there was a quick glimmer of recognition in Harvey Steinberg's eyes.

"I'd like to visit your center," he said.

Len did come into our program, and later went on to Bible school. Harvey Steinberg became a regular visitor at our center and soon volunteered his services—free.

One day Harvey came into my office waving a government check.

"I told you," he said triumphantly. "Not only are you tax-exempt, but here is a check for two thousand dollars—your tax money back."

There was another story behind the refund, too. Harvey had been finding it difficult to get into the office of the top administrator who would give the final okay on whether or not we would get any money back. Then one day his wife came home from her job as lab technician in a local hospital.

"Guess what," she said. "The man you've been trying to see about the taxes for Teen Challenge came to the lab today. I did some tests on him. When I found out who he was, I told him about Teen Challenge and how you're trying to help them. He said he would expedite the matter."

"You see," Harvey put the check on my desk, "I did it!"

The staff workers had gathered around and listened to the story; now they shouted loudly, "Praise the Lord; thank you,

Jesus!" until Harvey put his hands to his ears in mock exasperation.

"You people say 'Praise the Lord,' " he cried. "You should say, 'Thank you, Harvey.' "

God does things in His own way. A stranger walks in our door, a little old lady brings a paper bag, or a spinster schoolteacher gives her savings and our needs are met.

Sunday was smiling. "We're doing all right through the mail too," she said. "A Sunday school class in Oregon sends a love offering of seven dollars and thirty-four cents; some kids in Florida put on a chili supper and gospel sing and collect thirty-seven dollars; here is twenty-five dollars from a platoon of marines in Vietnam—they've seen our movie; and you'll never believe this one—twenty-five dollars in cash stuck in an envelope and postmarked Philadelphia. There's a note scribbled on a piece of wrapping paper: "with love from an acidhead who may need your help someday!"

I shook my head. It happened occasionally that a drug addict who rejected the gospel and walked out of our coffeehouse left a crumpled bill under a donut basket.

Frank, our supervisor of boys, walked past the door to Sunday's office trailed by two converts carrying mops and buckets. The last fellow was a new one—yet I thought I'd seen those heavy dark eyes before.

"Who?" I nodded toward the door.

"Ricky," Sunday said.

"But he walked away!" I remembered. "What happened?"

"Apparently his Dad decided to quit shielding him," Sunday explained. "When they left here Ricky went to a shooting gallery; his Dad trailed him and told the police. The place was raided and Ricky landed in jail. After a week in a cell where he kicked cold turkey, he was ready to ask the judge to put him into our custody. He came in four days ago, accepted Christ as his Savior the first evening and spent most of the night on his knees in the chapel crying to God. We could hear him all over the place. He received the Baptism in the Holy Spirit and praised God in tongues till dawn!"

"Thank you, Lord—and what else is new?" I said it jokingly, and Ona, who had just come in, started laughing.

"Guess who went to church with us Sunday?" she asked. I shook my head.

"Jimmy!"

"Jimmy who?"

"Jimmy from Hidden Manna, the fellow who's been torturing us for months. You know Kathy said she thought God was getting through to him."

Jimmy had turned up on the doorstep of our center Sunday morning, all ready to go to church. He was still wearing his jeans, white T-shirt, and beads, but he was clean.

"We told him he'd have to behave in church," Ona said, "and he really did. He said he wanted to quit drugs and get a job."

"Is he coming to the center?"

Ona shook her head. "No, he says he can do this thing on his own." She shrugged. "He's been down at the Square and at the coffeehouse again, and he still acts strange. Kathy is sure he'll come to the center to stay real soon. We'll just have to keep on praying."

XI

———————

WHILE our coffeehouse ministry was booming, we were learning to let God do the assigning of our workers to special posts. In the beginning we all pitched in and took turns doing everything. It soon became apparent that we could be far more efficient by letting the workers who did a certain thing best stay in that particular job.

Maureen and Todd had first come to us as children's workers, but like the rest of us they took turns being in charge of the Hidden Manna. Maureen had a way with children; she could walk down a sidewalk and soon have a following of little ones who jumped up and down and fought for a turn to hold her hand.

Todd was a tall, blond, ex-navy man who had met Christ as his Savior on a patrol boat off the coast of Vietnam. When he returned stateside he vowed to let God direct his life, and after a couple of years in Bible school found himself at Teen Challenge, Philadelphia.

He, too, had a way of walking down a street collecting a

trail of kids. Soon he was telling the kids in the neighborhoods to wait for him at a certain street corner at a certain hour, and he would tell them stories and teach them songs. The kids responded with enthusiasm, and all summer long Todd roamed the ghetto holding street-corner rallies for little kids.

I thought it was a good idea to keep Todd busy with the little ones. He could be quick-tempered at times, and tended to loose patience with teen-agers and long-time addicts. Four years in the navy had taught him the value of discipline. But he needed to learn that drug addicts cannot be expected to "snap to" at the first hint.

It was typical that Karen, in charge of the girls, and Frank, in charge of the boys, had to learn how to be firm, while Todd had to unlearn and temper the rigidness of his military training. Todd had to learn, too, that God does His work not by power, not by might, but by His Spirit.

How he learned is an amazing story in itself.

He had been assigned to the Hidden Manna one weekend. Four hippies who were quite obviously high on dope came in and began to heckle a couple of the girls. Todd stepped close, ready to punch the fellows and throw them out the door if necessary. Maureen shot him a warning glance and continued to talk calmly to the boys.

"Don't you know," she said sweetly, "that Jesus Christ is stronger than any power on earth? You can't hurt me."

One of the hecklers laughed loudly. "What if we drag you into an alley and shoot you up with an overdose of drugs? Can your Jesus keep you from dying?"

"Sure He can," Maureen smiled. "He has the power to neutralize any drug in the world. Haven't you guys noticed that you've had trouble staying high when you're in here talking about Jesus? That's the power of His Spirit."

The four guys looked at one another and moved uneasily.

"Look," one of them said. "That Jesus fellah has been dead for years; you're just kidding yourself."

Maureen only smiled and offered them more coffee, which they declined; they quickly ducked out the door.

"You should have let me throw those guys out," Todd said. "They're only looking for trouble."

"They're looking for Jesus," Maureen said. "They can't hurt me."

The following evening we were short of staff workers at the Hidden Manna. Our rules say that the workers go out in pairs to walk through the Square, talking to the people there and inviting them to visit the coffeehouse. Each pair is gone for half-an-hour. If they don't return on time, someone else goes out to find them.

Two girls who were new at the center had gone up to the Square, and the half hour went by without their return. Since we were short of workers at the coffeehouse, Todd reluctantly agreed to let Maureen go out alone to find the two missing girls. Todd was the only fellow working that evening; therefore he could not leave the coffeehouse himself.

The workers joined hands, prayed for Maureen's safety, and she left. The others calculated that it would take her five minutes to walk the two-and-a-half long blocks to the Square, perhaps five minutes to locate the girls, and another five minutes to return. After fifteen minutes the three of them were back. Maureen reported that all had gone well; she had walked without incident and without being spoken to. The two girls at the Square had simply forgotten to check their watches.

No sooner had Maureen and the others taken their places at the tables when the four hippies who had heckled our workers the night before came in. They headed for Maureen's table, and their leader blurted out, "Hey, Sis, who's your boyfriend? We didn't think you girls were supposed to walk with boys."

"I don't have a boyfriend," Maureen said quietly.

"Come off it," the others chimed in. "We saw you walking up to the Square with him just now. He's a good-looker—where'd you pick him up?"

Maureen shook her head. "I walked alone up to the Square; if you saw me, you know that's the truth."

The four hippies looked at each other, then at Maureen.

"Look, sister." The leader, a skinny little fellow with long hair, leaned over the table toward Maureen, and Todd automatically stepped closer to watch what was going on. "You Christians aren't supposed to lie. Maybe you don't want anybody to know about it, but we saw you walking with a guy. He was tall and blond and looked real strong." He looked at Todd, who stood six feet four. "Bigger than this guy here."

He leaned closer and looked Maureen intently in the eyes.

"You better thank him, too, 'cause we were waiting for you. We had the works ready and were gonna shoot you up with an overdose of heroin—just to show you that Jesus can't help you."

Maureen had grown pale at first; then a flush of color settled on her cheeks, and her eyes were aglow from within.

"Jesus did protect me, fellows," she said, her voice shaking just a little. "He sent an angel to walk with me to the Square.

I didn't see him; I just felt that I wasn't alone. But you saw him—you saw an angel!"

Wide-eyed, the four boys looked at one another; then without a word, they turned and left. Todd let out a long slow whistle and sat down at Maureen's table.

"Wow!" he said. "Did all those guys hallucinate at the same time?"

Maureen shook her head and smiled. "You prayed that God would send a guardian angel to watch over me, didn't you?" she asked.

Todd nodded. "Sure, but . . ."

"Didn't you expect Him to answer your prayer?"

"Well, not exactly *that* way—" Todd looked a little dubious, and Maureen continued patiently. "You believe that God has enough power to stop a mighty army if He so chooses, yet you seem to think He leaves all the fighting to us."

"Well," Todd grinned, "God helps those who help themselves—"

"Don't you know," Maureen went on, "that there's more power in the Holy Spirit than you could ever pack in a fist? You need to learn to call on that power and ask God to show you when to use your fist and when to let Him do the fighting. You know the scripture we're forever quoting from Zechariah 4:6: 'Not by might, nor by power, but by my spirit, saith the Lord of hosts'—and He was talking about leveling mountains!"

Todd looked thoughtful. "Do you think I'm too quick with my fists?"

Maureen nodded without speaking. "But what if a bunch of fellows surround you in an alley? If you don't fight, they'll do you in!" Todd insisted.

Maureen laughed. "Funny you should mention that," she said. "That happened to me one day."

During Maureen's first summer with us at the center she had walked into the black ghetto one day to tell the children about the story hour in our basement. She was walking down the street in an all-black neighborhood—just two or three blocks from our center—when suddenly she found herself surrounded by six muscular black youths. They seemed to come from nowhere—two walked in front of her, one on each side, and two in back. She was completely surrounded by their tight little squad.

Maureen continued down the sidewalk as if nothing had happened, ignoring their loud invitations to a "little lovin'."

"No, thank you," she said calmly. "I belong to Jesus, and He is walking with me right here. I'm not going with you; so why don't you run along?"

"C'mon, baby, we'll show you some real good stuff!" The fellows continued with their suggestions and began to reach out, touching Maureen. They were walking her down a side street now, and she was unable to break out of their tight circle. Ahead were stairs down to an open basement door. Another black boy was just going down carrying a case of beer, and the six fellows who were walking Maureen yelled out, "Hey, Joe, we got one. Look here!" The boy looked up, saw Maureen and grinned, rolling his eyes and letting out a long whistle.

Maureen knew she couldn't try running; they'd catch her and only have more fun out of the chase. "God," she prayed, "I know You're walking with me; please let those fellows know it too!"

Almost instantly the six stopped. Maureen looked up startled. Where he'd come from she didn't know, but directly in front of her stood a tall man. He said nothing, just stood there, his eyes looking into hers. The way she told it later, they were the kindest eyes she'd ever seen. They seemed to look way into her and give her strength. She suddenly felt as if she'd never been in a safer spot in her whole life.

When she looked around, the six fellows had run away. She saw the last of them disappear into the basement and heard the door slam. Then she turned and walked as quickly as she could back toward the center. She'd walked half a block before she remembered that she should have said "Thank you" to the man. She turned to look for him and saw nothing.

"Somehow I knew," she told Todd, "that God had sent an angel."

A few days later Todd was on duty in the coffee shop when three fellows came in, high on dope. Todd asked them politely to leave, but one grabbed a chair and tried to hit Todd. Instead, the chair smashed into bits against a post. This time Todd told the boys to get out, and two of them went willingly. The third turned in the doorway and promised to be back soon.

"I'll kill you," he told Todd.

Before long he was back, carrying a sharp piece of broken glass. Again Todd told him to leave, and he shouted, "Go ahead, try to hit me—I just want to cut your face up."

There were only a few customers and staff workers in the coffee shop; it was still early in the evening.

No one moved. The fellow with the broken glass was well known to our workers; he'd come in often and had seemed open to the news about Jesus Christ. Lately he'd begun to mainline speed, a drug that does exactly what the name says, speeds up every reaction, both physical and emotional. It can also make the addict super-paranoid and ready to turn on anyone at the slightest provocation.

Todd stood motionless, his fists opening and closing. He was staring the other fellow in the eye without saying a word.

"C'mon," the guy yelled. "You chicken or something? Let's see you fight!"

Todd didn't move, and a couple of the staff workers in the back began praying softly in the Spirit.

The fellow waved the broken glass a couple of inches in front of Todd's face. "I just want to cut your face up," he said. "Why don't you hit me?"

Suddenly Todd began praying out loud. He never moved his eyes from the other fellow; he just stood there, loudly thanking God for His shield of protection and for the presence of His Holy Spirit.

The fellow said, "Shut your eyes and pray."

Todd smiled and kept right on looking him in the eye and praying.

At last he said, "You can't cut me up even if you try—the power of God is preventing you."

The fellow looked like he was trying hard to move his hand with the broken glass in it closer to Todd's face. Cold sweat was breaking out on his forehead, and he looked suddenly terrified. Abruptly, he turned and ran out the door.

Todd came to the back of the coffeehouse and sat down. He told me later, "I could feel the power of the Holy Spirit so strong around me that I honestly don't think a bullet could have come through!"

Todd had learned his lesson about the superiority of God's

power over a ready fist. Some of the other workers had to learn the value of being ready to fight if necessary.

Frank, our supervisor of boys, found it hard to be firm. He'd come to Teen Challenge prepared to use a hammer and saw—he was trained in the building business. God could use his hammer and saw, but he had other plans for Frank too.

Being supervisor of boys is quite a job. It means assigning work to the converts and seeing that it gets done; it means taking the boys to the swimming pool, or down on the farm for a workout on the ball field, or escorting them to church almost every night. It also means being big brother and father confessor, seeing that lights are out and that everybody gets along with one another. The boys are at varying stages of rehabilitation, some fresh from the street or from jail, others getting ready to go on to college or a job on the outside.

Frank was a short fellow, and younger than many of the converts. They found it hard to take orders from him.

"What do I do, Bob?" Frank would come to my office. "I never know when I might get too abrupt and shake up a guy who is extra-sensitive." That had happened too. We'd had a couple of runaways who had gotten their feelings hurt and thought our rules were too hard. Whenever that happened, our staff workers would assemble in the chapel to search their own hearts and consciences to see if they had made a wrong step. Sometimes the trouble could be traced to an unfriendly word, or perhaps a worker had been busy with something else and ignored a convert who needed to talk or pray about a problem.

A nineteen-year-old convert named Chuck had a way of ignoring orders from the staff. Chuck was tall and strong, and he didn't have much respect for Frank.

I had talked to Chuck about obeying orders and showing respect for the staff, but I knew that sooner or later Frank would have to earn Chuck's respect himself.

Tension was growing in the men's dorm; everyone was aware of the silent battle of wills between Chuck and the supervisor. Little incidents were taking on a great deal of significance—a greasy comb left behind in the bathroom, a bed not properly made up, quiet snickering when Frank was unable to master the situation.

Chuck owned a pair of unusually heavy shoes. When he walked with deliberately heavy steps it sounded like a herd of elephants thundering across the floor.

One night Chuck was with a small group of the fellows who had stayed out late at a church service. Most of the boys were asleep in the dorm when they returned, and Frank told Chuck to please walk softly. Instead, Chuck walked the whole length of the floor making as much noise as he could, waking everybody up. They were yelling, "Be quiet!" but Chuck kept on walking.

Frank watched, then walked to where Chuck was standing and said, " I told you to walk softly. Why didn't you?"

Chuck looked around the dorm. Everyone was watching. He smiled broadly. "I'll do what I want to, when I want to, where I want to, and how I want to."

Quick as lightning Frank reached up and punched Chuck right in the face. The impact was so sudden that Chuck fell flat on his back. Frank reached down, pulled him back up, and threw him down on the bed.

"Stay there," he said flatly. "If I hear another word out of you I'll punch you through the wall."

Then Frank turned on his heel and ran downstairs to the chapel where he fell on his knees sobbing.

I happened to be there and listened to his confession, silently praising God under my breath.

"I don't know what came over me, Bob," Frank cried. "Before I knew it he was lying flat on his back looking dazed; I don't see how I got the strength to pick him up and throw him on that bed; he's almost twice my size. Oh, God! I sure didn't mean to lose my temper like that."

We prayed together, and I reminded Frank that even Jesus had gotten harsh with the money changers in the Temple.

Frank didn't look much relieved, but after an hour or so in the chapel he finally went to bed, convinced that even if he had made a mistake, God could surely use it for some good.

The next morning he came into my office, beaming.

"Would you believe that Chuck came over to my bed last night and *thanked* me for punching him? He said it was the first time anyone had ever crossed him; it had made him think, and he really saw himself as a bully. He said he was sorry for all the discord he'd caused in the dorm and asked me to pray with him about it."

XII

BY THE time we held our rally at the Chester center, Jimmy had been with us in church several Sundays. At the Hidden Manna he sometimes quoted the Bible to fellow addicts, but every so often the old Jimmy would show through and cause considerable havoc. You never knew how he was going to act.

Several of our workers and converts had felt concerned for Jimmy, concerned enough to spend hours on their knees in the chapel in intercessory prayer.

We've found that when a person cannot or will not pray, it is often possible for someone else to break through the barrier by praying for him. Jesus did this in Gethsemane; our workers often do it for a convert, sometimes with remarkable results.

When addicts are going through withdrawal, some of our workers read from the Bible and pray at the bedside while others pray in the chapel. There is a direct relationship between the amount of prayer and the lack of pain experienced by the addict in withdrawal.

When I say amount of prayer, of course I don't mean the

number of minutes or hours or words said. I'm talking about the power of God's Holy Spirit released through willing prayer-channels. The more you're a yielded prayer-channel, the more God is able to do His work through you.

Kathy had become a regular prayer-warrior, and Ricky was rapidly becoming one. Perhaps it was because both of them had been in need of much talking to God about their own problems.

Both Kathy and Ricky had been praying for Jimmy.

On the day of our big Chester rally, he showed up at the center, all ready to go along in the bus. As usual, he was dressed in his jeans, T-shirt, and beads.

The purpose of the rally was to raise money for the center.

Each of our branch centers is supposed to be self-supporting. Of course we are all working together, and the main center will help with support when it is necessary. Since ours is a faith work, we believe that God can meet the needs of all the centers directly.

I spoke at the rally and asked anyone in the audience who felt led by God to come forward and take an envelope. Within thirty days they were to send the envelope back to the center with twenty-five or fifty dollars enclosed.

One of the first to come forward was Jimmy. *God*, I thought, *Jimmy's carrying this funny-business too far. You know he's not reliable.*

I didn't want to embarrass Jimmy in front of everybody, so I gave him an envelope, certain that I'd never see it again.

A week later the envelope came back with fifty dollars enclosed—Jimmy's entire paycheck for that week. We rejoiced and thanked God.

Another week went by, and there was Jimmy at the door of our main center. He asked to see me.

"Reverend Bartlett," Jimmy looked serious, "I want to come into your program. I want to go all the way with Jesus."

That night in chapel he accepted Jesus Christ as his personal Savior—and received his "personal Pentecost," the Baptism in the Holy Spirit.

With each day it was clear that Jimmy meant business. When he first came, he had been hampered by stammering. Little by little his speech became perfect. Jimmy wanted to go all the way—into full-time service for Christ, whatever that would take and wherever it would lead.

We were all happy for him. In chapel his testimony was clear and strong; he was joining the rest of us wholeheartedly in our growing up together as a family in Christ.

Others didn't make the transition as easily. Corinna was a twenty-four-year-old black girl who had been on drugs for seven years. She came to us sick, but willing to be helped.

For two days and nights our workers sat with her, prayed with her, read the Bible, sang for her, and rubbed her body with dry towels when she had chills and cramps.

On the third day she was able to get up a little. Early in the afternoon she asked permission to take a shower. Kathy brought her clean clothes and went downstairs to join the other girls in the lounge.

They listened to the shower running and waited for it to stop. Corinna really wasn't strong enough to be left alone for long. She was coming along remarkably well, considering the fact that she had not accepted Christ as her Savior. Until she did, the drug habit would still have a strong emotional hold upon her.

Some of the boys were studying in the dining room. One of them appeared in the doorway of the girls' lounge to ask, "Did you leave a girl upstairs?"

"Yes," Karen said, "Corinna is taking a shower." The boy shook his head.

"I don't think she is now. Someone just walked through the dining room."

Kathy ran upstairs; the shower was running, but Corinna was not there.

In the kitchen a worker said she had tried to go out the back door, but he wouldn't let her.

They found her in the hall. She'd pulled the fire extinguisher off the wall and was heading for the front door screaming, "I want to get out of here—let me go!"

"Please don't, Corinna," Karen said soothingly. "You're not very strong yet."

"I want to leave—let me go!" Corinna shook the doorknob.

"Okay." Karen said firmly. "You are free to go—but first I want God to do something for you."

Suspicious but subdued, Corinna allowed the girls to lead her upstairs. I was called, and we all came together in the chapel.

We knew full well that nothing we could say would make any difference for Corinna now. Only the power of God could change her. So we gathered around, laid hands on her, and began to pray. Almost immediately she fell to her knees, sobbing. While we continued praying, she began to cry out to God for help, asking Him to forgive her and make her whole.

When she finally stood up, Corinna was transformed. Her eyes were shining and she laughed.

"I'm not leaving," she said. "Thank God I didn't get away!"

Some did get away. Some did it dramatically, like Maggie, who slid down a rope from the roof and tore open the insides of her hands in the process. We caught her, brought her to the doctor, kept her till she healed, and then she walked away. Our program is voluntary. Sometimes I wish it wasn't. But there is nothing we can do when an addict doesn't want help.

Cissy was like Corinna in many ways. She had been on dope for five years and was in bad shape when she came to us. The first night at the center she nearly died. We called Dr. Cohill in the middle of the night. Cissy weighed only seventy-four pounds when she came in; she had had a baby four months earlier, and her body was simply wasted away.

Withdrawal was painful for Cissy. The cramps would get her; she'd run the floor like a wild animal, ready to lunge at anyone who tried to hold her.

After a week she was doing better. Still, the cramps in her legs would make her scream out in pain, and she had difficulty walking. We prayed for her, but so far she had refused to ask God for help.

Then one day she attempted to run away. We caught her trying to break the glass in our front door. Finally she was persuaded to come with us to the chapel. "If you let us pray for you, we'll let you go later," I promised. Cissy agreed, but only because she wanted to get out and get a cigarette. For some reason, the hunger for a cigarette can be the stumbling block for an addict trying to kick the habit.

In the chapel we gathered around and laid hands on Cissy. "Oh, God," I prayed. "Show Cissy Your love for her; heal her pain." Instantly we could feel something like an electric current come through our hands and into Cissy's thin body. She fell to the floor and laid there looking astonished.

"Cissy, I know God can deliver you." I knelt next to her. "We want you to stay."

Slowly she sat up and moved first one leg, then the other.

"The pain is gone, isn't it," I said, and Cissy nodded reluctantly. "I still don't want to stay," she said. "I want a cigarette. My pain just went away by itself. It wasn't God."

This time we couldn't stop her. She had a free will. The choice was hers. God had shown His healing power, and she had refused to believe.

We cried that night in the chapel. Cissy walked out our front door and we never heard from her again.

Addicts who come to us directly from the street are often victims of a number of diseases in addition to their drug problem. Many suffer from malnutrition, hepatitis, or venereal disease. Before we admit them into our program they get a complete physical checkup. Many need to be under a doctor's care or observation during their first few weeks with us.

From the start, a Christian doctor offered to care for our unwed mothers and the female members of our staff during pregnancy and delivery. Several of our God Squad young couples have growing families.

The medical expenses for our addicts were high. It was difficult to find a doctor who was willing to make a house call in the middle of the night to the bedside of a drug addict in the throes of withdrawal.

God had provided us with the funds to pay our doctor and hospital bills, but we were still praying that somehow a Christian doctor would come along and feel the call to help us.

Our Tuesday night chapel services are open to visitors, and often strangers walk in from the street. One night I noticed a well-dressed young man in his early thirties. He had come alone and did not seem to know anyone. Toward the end of our service he stood up to speak.

"I'm a doctor," he said. "God has just impressed me to offer my services here at the center."

I found out that Doctor Donald Cohill was a Presbyterian who very recently had come to experience what is recorded in the New Testament as the Baptism in the Holy Spirit. He had turned his life and future career over to God, and was presently serving on the staff of a nearby hospital.

Dr. Cohill became a part-time member of the God Squad, but he joined us full-time in spirit and enthusiasm for the work and for Christ.

At first he examined his Teen Challenge patients on an old kitchen table in the center; later he donated an examination table, three hospital beds, and other supplies. Former drug addicts have to go easy on medication that might become habit-forming, but what medicines we needed, Dr. Cohill supplied without cost. All of us got free flu shots and vaccinations. Every two weeks Dr. Cohill would hold a clinic at the center. He'd arrive at 7 p.m. and often work till after midnight.

Many hospitals and rehabilitation centers are now letting addicts withdraw from drugs more or less cold turkey—with a minimum of medication or none at all. Cold turkey is becoming an accepted thing, but still, authorities are reassured when we tell them that we have a doctor on twenty-four-hour emergency call, and that everyone who comes to us has a physical examination before being admitted.

God even provided us with a nurse.

I was speaking at a college in the Midwest, and a young girl came forward after the meeting, red-eyed and shaken.

"Brother Bartlett," she said, "I was certain God had called me to be a nurse. Why do I feel this strong compulsion to come to Teen Challenge?"

"Let's pray about it," I suggested. "Maybe God needs a nurse in Philadelphia."

"I've already been accepted in an overseas training program for the mission field," she said. "God doesn't change His mind, does He?"

I shook my head. "Did you ask God if He wanted you in that program?" I asked, and she blushed slightly.

"I just wanted to go very much," she said. "I assumed God wanted it too."

"Look," I told her. "We've been praying that God would send us someone with a background in nursing. But I wouldn't want you to come just for that reason. I want you to pray until you know for sure where God wants you to be. We don't want just any nurse, we want the one nurse in the whole world whom God is calling to Teen Challenge."

She smiled through tears. "I'll pray about it some more," she said. "I'll let you know."

I already knew, and sure enough, three weeks later a letter came from Marsha. She said that if we needed her she would come as soon as the semester was over.

We thanked God for the great things He was doing at the center, but there were still more problems I thought He ought to be solving. The question about a separate residence for girls kept coming up. It wasn't easy to work with converts of both sexes under one roof when they really needed to be separated.

They come to us with the same hang-ups, and on the out-side they've often run in the same gangs. You see them on the streets, the girls in jeans, the boys with long hair—and can't tell the difference unless you look closely.

Yet many more boys come to us for help than girls. The girls who come are more despondent than the boys; they have a far more hopeless attitude, as if they consider themselves somehow more sinful than the boys. Girls often have a hang-up on sex, and many of them are so confused and so full of ha-tred for themselves and for the world that they have become either prostitutes or lesbians.

Girls' rehabilitation often takes longer, and the girls need more attention, more consistent counseling and help. Girls are also more conscious of their surroundings. We had prayed that God would meet our need and find a place that would be beautiful as well as practical.

Several times Ona and I had gone to look for a house. We'd gone so far as to make bids, but something always got in the way. We usually ended up on our knees in the chapel, ask-ing God to forgive us that we'd run ahead of Him again, promising that we would try to be more patient in the future.

One day there was a call from a realtor. There was a house in Germantown. Would we like to look at it? Sure we would.

The house was really a small mansion: seven bedrooms, large living rooms, dining room, spacious kitchen—and all surrounded by beautiful grounds. Lots of trees, wide lawns. It belonged to an old lady who had been operating a boarding house. She wanted to sell it with the furniture, which meant all the beds we needed.

We loved it, but it was very near the mansion we'd first looked at when we wanted to start our center, the mansion

God wouldn't let us have. The same zoning laws were in effect, and the same zoning board. Would we like to make an offer? Sure, anything, but there really wasn't much hope.

We especially liked the idea of seven bedrooms. Many girls come to us with lesbian problems, and we are very reluctant to take them in. Trying to rehabilitate them in a crowded girls' dorm is much like trying to wean an alcoholic in a bar.

For a long time we didn't accept any lesbians at all. We honestly didn't know of any who had been cured. I'm not talking about girls who have played around with it. I'm talking about hard-core practicing lesbians who have chosen this as a way of life.

Then Sophia came. She was a slender twenty-two-year-old dressed like a man, with her hair cut short.

"Look, man," she said, shrugging her shoulders, "I do my thing and you do yours. I don't see how that can be wrong."

"So why did you come to us?" Ona asked.

Sophia nodded toward her mother. "She thinks I ought to change my ways; just for her sake I'd be willing to give it a try."

Ona shook her head. "Sorry, Sophia," she said. "We can't let you come in. You're not going to live here with our girls as long as you think 'your thing' is all right. God calls 'your thing' a sure sign of complete degradation. Read the first chapter of Romans; Paul talks about it there."

Sophia looked a little bored. "I know what the Bible says," she said. "I grew up with the Book. But we live in a different age. Homosexuality isn't wrong—it's just different; it certainly doesn't hurt anybody."

Ona looked at Sophia's mother. "I'm sorry," she said. "We can't possibly help your daughter. No one can, until she understands that she needs help. We can't help drug addicts either, unless they really get desperate and disgusted with their own condition. When Sophia gets to that point, call us, and we'll be glad to talk to her any time of the day or night."

When the mother and daughter had left, Ona turned to me.

"Let's pray," she said. "I have a feeling about that girl. At least she's very honest about her condition, and that could be a first step. Let's pray that the Holy Spirit will lift that blindness from her so that she can see herself as God would see her."

Sophia was made a special prayer target for the next several days. Ona was right—honesty is a necessary takeoff point. We've had girls come here for help who tried to hide the fact that they were lesbians. Sooner or later it would become evident, and we had to ask them to leave—not because they were lesbians, but because they lied about it.

I remember Tessi, a tall blonde girl from the Northwest. She came in with a drug problem, and after a couple of weeks we knew that she was a lesbian. Karen called her aside and asked her if she had any personal or emotional problems she hadn't discussed with us yet. Tessi shook her head. "Not that I know of," she said brightly. "I'm doing fine, thank you."

"Have you ever had any problems in your personal relationship with other people?" Karen asked. Again Tessi shook her head.

"Nope," she said.

"Ever become too attached to a girl friend?" Karen asked. Tessi looked a bit startled, but still persisted in saying no.

Karen brought her to Ona; and together they told Tessi that they knew what her problem was, and that we could help her if she'd just admit it.

"Jesus Christ died for all our sins and hang-ups," Ona said. "He can forgive you and help you with your problem too." Tessi got very angry and stalked out of the office saying it was none of their business how she lived her private life.

Soon Tessi was gone.

Homosexuality is no longer a hush-hush subject, but it is still a touchy one. Yet if we read the Bible we see that it was very common in New Testament times. It was, indeed, one of the symptoms of a sick society. It was very prevalent in Rome before the fall of that empire. In the New Testament the Apostle Paul discusses it very frankly in his letter to the Romans in the first chapter, and it was obviously a problem in Corinth too.

The week following Sophia's visit to our center, I was gone on a speaking tour. Late one night Ona returned home to find a message: "Urgent, call Sophia's mother!"

Ona called, and the voice at the other end was almost incoherent.

"Please!" she sobbed. "Sophia has cried for three days. She's desperate and wants help. Can I bring her?"

Ona was hesitant. Sophia could be putting on a show— that's happened before—and she hated to make a decision about letting her come to the center while I was out of town.

"Please, at least talk to her." The mother was crying.

"All right," Ona said, "you can bring her right away. I'll talk to her, but I won't promise to let her into our program."

The time was midnight. It would take the mother and daughter an hour to drive to Philadelphia from the small town where they lived. Ona called Sunday and Karen, and the three of them knelt together in prayer.

"God, You know Sophia's heart," Ona prayed. "If You're

the One who's made a change in her, let us see it. If she's faking it, give us the insight to know that too. Help us not to rely on our own understanding, but to trust and obey Your voice."

The Sophia who walked into the center a few minutes later was very different from the cocksure, self-satisfied creature who had walked away the week before.

Her pretty features were swollen almost beyond recognition by days and nights of crying. She was dressed in a pair of old faded jeans and a sweat shirt, and her slender fingers were continually folding and unfolding a moist handkerchief.

"I need help," she cried, and Ona looked at her calmly. "Why?" she asked.

"I hate myself like this." Sophia began to sob uncontrollably. "Oh God, I hate it."

"What happened?" Ona looked at the mother who put an arm around her daughter's shoulders in an effort to console her.

"I guess I started it," she said. "Sophia had come to stay with me between 'affairs.' She always does that, and I've never said anything about it. I always thought that if I didn't condemn her or criticize her, maybe she'd accept my love and change some day."

The mother looked at Sophia and continued. "But last week, when some of my friends were coming for coffee, I looked at my daughter, and suddenly I loathed what I saw. I knew that her closet was full of men's clothing, and that soon she'd move into an apartment with a girl and be her lover. The thought made me nauseated and sick with shame. When my friends arrived, I introduced Sophia as a stranger, as if she was only a casual acquaintance who happened to be at my house. When they left, Sophia asked why I hadn't told them who she was. I looked straight at her, and for the first time in my life admitted that I was ashamed of her, that I was sick of the way she lived, that I was sorry she was my daughter. She stared at me openmouthed, without a word, then turned and ran to her room."

Silent tears were running down the mother's cheeks; Sophia's head was on her shoulder.

"I thought I did right in shielding her," the mother said. "Instead, by hiding my honest reactions from her, I kept her from being honest with herself. I am as much in need of God's forgiveness as my daughter is."

Ona, Karen, and Sunday looked at one another. God had answered prayer.

"If you forgive each other, and then ask God to forgive you, He is faithful and just, and does it," Ona said. "I believe God has begun His work in Sophia, and He will continue it. She has a hard road ahead, but with God's help she'll make it."

Sophia looked up; there was a glimmer of light in her eyes. "Will you help me?"

Ona nodded. "We'll help you seek God's help," she said.

It wasn't easy to counsel with Sophia. We made it a rule never to let any one counselor deal with her any longer than a few weeks at a time, because of her tendency to form strong attachments to special friends.

Sophia was helped. It didn't come easy, but it came. She spent much time in prayer and in memorizing the Word of God—her most effective weapon against temptation.

After a week at the center she received the Baptism in the Holy Spirit. Jesus called that, "the Power from on High"; and soon afterward Sophia decided to commit herself to full-time work for God. She spent nearly a year with us, then went to Bible college. Ona had a letter from her recently; she was working in a mission on an Indian reservation.

Sophia was helped, and we learned that in Jesus Christ nothing is impossible; no addiction or perversion or sin is immune to the power of His Blood.

Because of Sophia we learned that lesbians can be helped.

Because of Sophia we prayed that God would give us the mansion in Germantown.

XIII

RICHARD and Danny did much of the planning for our summer street work. Our street meetings were centered around music and personal testimonies of former addicts. Both were essential, and God had certainly provided us with young people who could sing and tell others what God was doing in their lives.

Three times a week during the summer, some of our people hold a meeting on the Boardwalk at Atlantic City. During our first summer in Philadelphia, a minister from Atlantic City had invited us to hold meetings on the beach.

Richard and Danny put together a program of singing and testimonies that drew thousands of listeners on the Boardwalk. The response was tremendous.

Of course, all the listeners aren't enthusiastic. There have been hecklers and scoffers, but it is funny how God can turn the worst possible situation into a demonstration of His power and perfect control.

One hot summer evening the entire choir had been singing

and witnessing at the Boardwalk. The nights when the whole choir is there, the group of listeners often grows to a thousand or more during the evening. Our choir has contributed excellent music, and Richard attributes as much to the power of prayer as to rehearsals. In fact, when the choir members meet for rehearsal, they usually spend at least as much time on their knees praying for each other and for their listeners as they do singing.

I've come into the chapel during rehearsal and heard a choir member suddenly speak up to ask for prayer for a sore throat, or headache, or depression; and the other choir members will gather around to lay on hands and to pray. I've watched the rehearsals break into periods of exuberant prayer and praise to God.

The results have been amazing. Our choir has sung at services where the presence and power of the Holy Spirit has literally descended upon the listeners during the singing.

Richard says, "It isn't that we have great voices; it's just that we're singing in the Name of Jesus Christ and by His Power. His Spirit does the rest."

On that hot summer evening at the Boardwalk we had noticed a large group of young fellows moving restlessly on the edge of the crowd. Some of our workers who were there to hand out literature got nowhere when they tried to talk to them. They were quite obviously hanging around just waiting for trouble.

We closed the meeting at ten and started walking toward our cars. Our group was large—some of the fellows walked ahead, the girls were in the center, and the rest of the fellows brought up the rear. We hadn't noticed the hecklers for a while and thought they had left.

Suddenly they appeared, some of them drunk and armed with knives, and attacked the group of fellows walking up ahead. The attackers knocked some of the boys to the ground and kicked them in the face; then they walked through the group of girls—without so much as looking at them or touching them—and jumped on the rear group of our fellows. Richard was in the group. He was carrying a stack of music and happened to have turned around to face the fellow walking behind him. One of the attackers spun him around, cursed, and said, "You're the one who directs those Holy Rollers—I don't like you at all!" With that he hit Richard and sent him flying backward through the air while the music scattered all around.

Miraculously, none of our crew was seriously hurt. The police came on the scene and caught twelve of the guys before they could get away. I was asked to come down to the police station to press charges.

At the station I told the officer in charge that I did not want to press charges, but that I would like an opportunity to talk to the twelve culprits. They were marched in to stand in line facing me. They looked sullen and uneasy. I told them we would not press charges; that brought a spark of interest to their eyes.

"It isn't because I've got a lot of sympathy for you guys and want to see you get off easy," I said. "You know we're from Teen Challenge, and you call us Holy Rollers. But we serve a mighty and just God who loves you so much that He sent His son Jesus Christ, not to condemn you, but to pay for your wrongdoings on the cross and offer you freedom and peace instead. All you have to do is receive Him." The twelve were looking at me, but I couldn't tell if what I said made an impression.

"We're not going to press charges," I continued, "but I'm asking every one of you to be honest with God about what you're doing. You confess your sins to Him and He doesn't put you in a jail cell, He gives you a new life in Christ." They stood in silence; I saw tears glisten in the eyes of a long-haired skinny kid.

"You know our address in Philadelphia," I said, "1620 Broad Street. We're in the phonebook too. Anytime you need help, call us. Jesus loves you; He doesn't turn anyone down."

I turned and walked out of there, trusting that somehow God had made Himself known to those kids. We had suffered a few bruises; so what?—if even one rebel had caught a glimpse of God's forgiving love.

That night there was rejoicing as we gathered in the chapel for our midnight communion service.

Our days start at 7 a.m. with prayer and meditation, and our summer staff works all day and late into the evening before returning to the center. I am convinced that the only reason we can keep going on that kind of schedule without collapsing from sheer exhaustion is the source of our strength—God's Holy Spirit. I once told a panel of educators and social workers about our summer schedule, and one of them asked, "Do you mean to say that after working all those hours the young people aren't permitted to go to bed, but have to stay up for an extra hour taking communion and worshiping in the chapel?"

I smiled and said, "We get to the communion service completely exhausted, but after an hour of worship and breaking bread, some of our workers are ready to go back out on the streets to witness some more. We get our rest and strength from God, not just by sleeping."

Some of our workers *do* go back into the streets after midnight, and often we have found dope addicts or some miserable lonely soul ready to commit suicide in the night. They are willing to pour out their troubles to our workers and ask for help. One unwed mother who was brought to our center in the early morning hours said, "You people must really care, or you wouldn't walk the streets all night just to keep me from dying."

Our midnight communion service becomes a time of restoring strength, rejoicing in God's care, and praying for the young people we've met during the day. Sometimes workers stay on in the chapel in intercessory prayer until dawn.

The night after the Boardwalk incident the phone rang at the center at 1 a.m. I answered and heard a young man's voice, shaking with sobs.

"Mr. Bartlett," he cried, "I heard you talk in jail last night. I need Jesus. Can I come to your center?"

"Sure!" Gratitude welled up in me. "Are you an addict?"

"Yes." His voice was shaking. "I've been freaking out on speed, but I'm crashing now. I need help."

Terry was the skinny kid with the long hair. We put him on the scales, and he checked in at 78 pounds. He'd been taking dope for seven years, starting with pot at fourteen, graduating to LSD when he was fifteen.

"I was a senior in high school then," he said. "I was kind of serious and used to read a lot—philosophy and religion and that stuff—and I got to hanging around with a bunch of kids at the University who were a lot older than me. Then Timothy Leary came to the University and told us about the Neo-American Church he was forming. I got interested and went backstage to take some of the LSD.

From the Neo-American Church Terry "graduated" to a hippie camp in the New England woods where they studied Thoreau and Zen Buddhism and experimented with every drug they could buy or concoct.

"I started going down then," Terry confessed. "I got strung out on speed and got so paranoid I could see cops with machine guns coming after me everywhere. I ran into the woods and saw lots of little green men who wanted me to come live with them underground."

He started hitchhiking up and down the east coast, and in a big city came across a small band of Satan Worshippers.

"Till then I'd been seeking the light," Terry said. "Now I discovered how real the powers of darkness were, and I became a sorcerer's apprentice. I even had my own guardian demon I could conjure up at will."

Terry had arrived in Atlantic City a few weeks ago, had slept under the Boardwalk, and had been drawn to listen to our meetings.

"Like I wanted to destroy you people," he cried, tears running down his bony cheeks. "I knew Jesus was for real, and He was the enemy I was supposed to destroy; but every time I got near your stand and heard you singing about the Blood of Jesus, my head started pounding, and I got pains all over, and I knew Satan was gonna kill me."

We took Terry into the chapel and gathered around to

pray, knowing that God alone could break the bonds to set Terry free.

From that moment, Terry made amazing strides forward —physically, emotionally, and spiritually. It was as if God had seen that he was so totally broken-down in body and spirit that he needed an extra dose of supernatural strength from above.

Terry spent every spare minute studying the Bible, always coming up with gems he had to share with the rest of us.

"Look," he said triumphantly one morning, waving his copy of *Good News for Modern Man*. "Look what it says in II Corinthians 12:9. God says, 'My grace is all you need; for my power is strongest when you are weak, I am most happy, then, to be proud of any weaknesses, in order to feel the protection of Christ's power over me.'" Terry beamed. "That's me, man," he said. "Praise God, that's me!"

Terry felt that God had called him to become a minister, and before the summer was over, he was back down on the Boardwalk at Atlantic City, this time behind the microphone on our stand.

"Listen to me," his voice boomed over the Boardwalk. "I know God is for real, 'cause I've tried every counterfeit in the book."

And some were satisfied with counterfeits . . .

The day had been hot and the night was balmy. The Boardwalk was crowded and noisy, the neon lights glaring, and the rock music blasting from the shooting galleries and penny arcades.

One of our trios was singing. Ona and I walked away from the crowd to sit on the steps leading down to the beach. Across the stretch of sand was the vast darkness of ocean blending into black sky in the distance. A light breeze was blowing a whiff of salt fresh air from the sea. Ona breathed deeply and leaned her head against the wooden fence.

The surf looked frosty white between the sand and the sea; the sound was a steady beat behind the noises from the Boardwalk.

"God made the boundaries of the sea," Ona said dreamily. "Stormy or calm, the ocean cannot move beyond the limits God makes. Even so with our lives—when we give ourselves into His hands, He won't let us go beyond the boundaries He sets."

"When we yield," I agreed. "The problem is when we don't, and the restlessness and storms of our lives overflow and wash away everything we've tried to build up."

A girl was walking alone across the sand toward us. We both saw her at once—it was as if she had come up out of the surf. Long, windblown hair, a thin figure with a knitted shawl thrown around her shoulders—even in the warm night she looked chilled. As we watched her come barefoot across the sand, we realized there was something familiar about her. She wore large metal-rimmed sunglasses and swayed lightly, as if the wind was about to blow her down.

I heard Ona draw a sharp breath. "Candy!"

The girl stopped, then waved a thin arm and ran clumsily across the sand. "Ona! Bob! Wow! How are you?" She sat down on the step below us and folded her arms around her knees. Her smile was bright, but there were telltale lines in the thin face, and her long hair was unwashed and uncombed.

"How are *you*, Candy?" Ona asked.

Candy laughed. "I'm just great, everything is beautiful, man."

"Where have you been?" I asked.

Candy drew suddenly sober and put her head down on her knees. "It's been a bad trip," she said. "I went to Appalachia to work with those poor people." She tossed her head and looked up at me. "Man, those poor kids, those babies, they don't have any shoes in the snow, and they are starving to death. And what's God doing about it?"

"Why did you leave there?" Ona asked.

Candy shook her head. "Like it broke my heart to look at those kids and God wasn't doing anything." Her voice rose in anger. "Those babies haven't done anything wrong! Why does God punish them—what kind of God is He anyway? You tell me!"

Ona put her hand on Candy's shoulder. "You used to know what kind of God He is," she said softly. "He sent Jesus, didn't He?"

"Oh yeah?" Candy laughed. "What's Jesus doing about it?"

"What are *you* doing about it?" Ona asked.

"Me?" Candy laughed again. "What am *I* supposed to do? —I'm not God or Jesus."

"God sent you to Appalachia," I reminded her. "Jesus said whatever you do to one of these little ones you do to Him, and Jesus promised to be with us. Do you think you're helping those little kids by copping out and wandering around on the beach high as a kite?"

"Look," Candy was angry, "I didn't ask your opinion of me—I'm doing all right. Religion was a bum trip, and man, I've found my own kind of peace."

"In a needle?" Ona asked it quietly.

"So what?" Candy laughed brightly. "It's for real, and it's beautiful; you ought to try it sometime. I never did feel like this when I was trying to get hung up on Jesus. You guys really did your best, but it never got to be real, man."

"Why didn't it, Candy?" I asked, remembering that even while Candy had been with us, singing duets with Kathy, there had been a shrill emptiness behind her laughter; her joy had seemed forced, her restlessness still with her.

" 'Cause I just didn't want to be a puppet for anybody, not even Jesus. No one gets to own me, man. I'm free. I can turn this thing on and off. You guys are all sold out to God, and I just value my freedom too much, that's all."

We sat in silence. I saw the tears glisten in Ona's eyes as she watched Candy's slender fingers twist the ends of her shawl. The nails had been bitten halfway down, and her hands were dirt-stained.

We could hear Danny's voice over the microphone: ". . . Friends, you either belong to God or you're in the hands of Satan—there is no in-between . . . Where are you tonight, friend?"

Candy leaned her head back and laughed. "Good old Danny," she said. "I'm way ahead of all of you. Like my mind is so big that the whole world fits right into it, and I'm speeding so fast I'm getting to the end of the world way ahead of Jesus." She chuckled to herself and drew a circle in the sand with her big toe. "See the hole? I'm Alice in Wonderland and White Rabbit is taking me to a tea party, and we're not going to be late this time."

Ona put her hand on Candy's shoulder.

"Please, Candy," she said. "Jesus loves you and we love

you. You're going to kill yourself if you don't get off that stuff."

Candy stood up. "I've got to go," she said. "Tell Jesus I love Him too, but like I'm going my way this time." She waved two fingers in the air. "Peace, man, peace."

We watched her turn and go back across the sand, her footprints wavering.

Danny had stopped talking. Over the loudspeaker came the soft strumming of a guitar, then Kathy's deep mellow voice. "The Lord gave His love to me, when I was just a rebel . . ." We watched Candy stop, as if frozen in her tracks. How often she and Kathy had sung that song together!

"The Lord shed His blood for me . . . Now He bears all my burdens . . . The love I feel in my heart, the joy that overflows, I found the way, I found the truth, I found the light. Praise the Lord. My heart was made anew."

Slowly Candy continued walking away toward the surf, the wind blowing her hair and the ends of her shawl.

Ona took my hand, her voice choked with tears.

"Oh, God," she whispered. "Have mercy on her soul."

XIV

FRANK looked at me resolutely.

"I *have* prayed about it, Bob," he said. "God is telling me that He brought Marsha here to be my wife."

I walked to the window and looked up at the sky.

"Look, Frank," I said patiently. "Marsha has been here for two months. If you've been true to our rules, you have never been on a date with her or spoken to her in private." I turned to face Frank. "Or have you broken our rules?"

Frank shook his head.

"Then how do you *know* she's to be your wife? Have you asked her?"

"I've prayed and prayed," Frank said, "for the Lord to send me the right girl, and I asked that He would let me know for certain when she came along." Frank looked at me. "I told God I didn't want to make a mistake; I wanted Him to chose my wife. I know it's Marsha."

"Have you asked her?" I persisted, and Frank shook his head but looked undaunted.

"I'm sure God has spoken to her also," he said. "I'm asking your permission to speak to her alone."

"Would you mind telling me what God has shown you—to make you feel this certain about a girl you've never even been alone with?" I asked, and Frank grinned widely.

"You know I've given my life to God," he said. "I told God I needed a wife to work alongside me, and for a long time I've had real peace inside about that. I knew what she would have to be like—fully committed to God, someone I could work with and pray with." Frank laughed a little. "You know I never did think what she ought to look like. I figured God knew best what I would be happy with—only I didn't think He'd pick a girl quite as beautiful as Marsha!"

I shook my head and couldn't help laughing with him. There was no doubt about the gleam in Frank's eye. He was in love.

"Maybe I haven't talked to Marsha much," he said. "But I've watched her these two months. I've worked next to her, sometimes late at night when she's washed the sores of a drug addict, or spent hours on her knees with a convert who needed prayer. Marsha isn't up one day and down the next; she isn't moody or selfish. I've seen her share her food when we've been short; I've seen her smile and offer to help another worker when she's been up half the night and probably needed her rest."

Frank looked serious. "I'm not going on feelings, Bob," he said, "honestly I'm not. You can get fooled by feelings. I've been checking on the facts. I want to marry the girl God has picked for me, and I know that all the facts have got to stack up, or we'll spend the next fifty years together in a living hell."

"Okay, Frank," I gave in. "I just wanted to make sure you

weren't carried away. You may talk to Marsha alone—once."
I smiled. "If she says 'yes' you'll have to make plans to take a
leave of absence till the wedding. You know we don't make
any exceptions to our rules for dating—not even for couples
who are engaged."

Marsha and Frank weren't the first couple who had met at
Teen Challenge, in spite of our rigid rules. Or maybe rules
had nothing to do with it. The couples who met and married
had come here in response to God's calling them, and God
knew very well what He was doing when He brought them together.

Our God Squad couples are happier than most young people I've ever met, although they live on pennies and often in
cramped quarters with very little privacy—exactly the condi-
tions most marriage counselors would say were dangerous to
the success of a marriage.

Frank talked about basing a marriage on facts rather than
feelings, and the facts to which he referred had nothing to do
with a bank account or liking the same kind of music. They
did have something to do with Jesus Christ. He knew that
when both partners in a marriage had committed themselves
to go where He wants them to go and do what He wants them
to do, then they could eat beans and sleep on a straw mattress
in a mud hut in Africa, and know more joy and excitement
than all the money in the world could get them.

Frank asked permission to take Marsha to the zoo. He
thought if I'd give them two hours they could settle the matter
about marriage. I consented, and one bright day in early fall
the two of them took off on their first date. Frank told me later
he had proposed while they were feeding peanuts to the ele-

phant, and Marsha had asked if they could please pray about it before she gave her answer. They had knelt together on a green patch of lawn, asking God to have His way and show them His perfect will. Then they stood up. Marsha looked at Frank and said simply, "Praise the Lord, I really love you!" and it was settled.

They came to tell me, and Frank agreed to leave for his home state the next week. He would spend a few months preaching in a small church there and arrange support for himself and his new bride when they would return to Teen Challenge. Marsha would stay on at the center till a week before the wedding.

When Danny and Judi had moved into the run-down brownstone house in Kensington, I knew that the adjustment would be hard for Judi to make. To live on faith smacked of taking charity from hard-working churchgoers back home, and Judi's pride was taking a blow.

"We work twelve and fourteen hours a day," Danny had told her. "God provides everything we need. What more can we ask?"

"I just want to know what we're going to make next month," Judi explained, "so that I can put a little bit aside for some new curtains or maybe save enough for a piece of linoleum."

"Let's pray about it, honey." Danny took her hands in his. "God knows our needs."

The next day a neighbor walked into Judi's kitchen. She held a roll of cloth under her arm.

"I hope you won't feel bad about it," she told Judi, "but

someone gave me this material, and I just don't know what to do with it. I hate to let it go to waste? Can you use it?"

The material was exactly the color Judi had dreamed about for her living room curtains, and it fit the size of the windows—to the inch!

That same day at the center, some of our boys were cleaning out a storage room in the basement. They found a roll of linoleum that had never been used. Someone suggested that Danny might need it. He brought it home, and it just happened to fit their kitchen floor!

Still, there was much to be done before the apartment would look like a cozy home. The former tenants had put up so many layers of wallpaper that it was impossible to paint. The paper hung in shreds, and it would be necessary to tear it all down and redo the walls. Danny and Judi just didn't have the money to hire it done.

"Oh, Danny," Judi complained, "all I want is to make a nice house for you to come home to. Is that asking too much?"

Danny had been trying to tear down the layers of wallpaper; now he threw the tools on the floor and took Judi by the hand.

"Let's go for a walk," he said. "Let's get out of here for a while."

They walked down their block and past the next one. It was dark, and in the houses people had turned on the lights. Through the windows Danny and Judi could see into neat-looking living rooms, warm and friendly and comfortable-looking.

"Oh, Danny," Judi squeezed his hand, "I don't really care what the apartment looks like—as long as we're doing what God wants us to do."

"But I think God cares," Danny said, taking longer steps, suddenly hurrying. "I'm going to ask Him for a sign. If He wants us there, I'll ask that He give us fifty dollars to fix up the place. I'm going to ask Him to give it to us by tomorrow night at midnight."

They started running down the sidewalk, still holding hands, laughing excitedly. Back at the apartment Danny looked at the multicolored layers of torn wallpaper and laughed.

"Praise the Lord!" he said. "God, we thank You for the miracle You're going to do for us."

The next evening Danny and Judi were scheduled to sing and give their testimonies in a small church on the outskirts of Philadelphia. They went there confident that God would give them fifty dollars in the offering. When the plate was returned and the money counted, it came to only $8.73, and the deacon said they would mail it to the center later.

Stunned, Danny and Judi looked at each other. They had been so certain.

Back in Kensington, Judi went to bed, and Danny sat in the darkened living room staring at the shadows on the wall. The clock on the wall said 11:55. Danny felt the hopelessness of everything closing in. What had he brought Judi into? He had promised to provide and care for her, and now this—a ramshackle house with wallpaper in shreds, never knowing where the next meal would come from . . .

The phone rang.

That night I had spoken at a large rally in the city. The offering for our center was what we needed—and then some. I was delighted. On my way home in the car, I had a persistent thought—Danny and Judi need help! I didn't know their financial situation. Each worker was responsible for his own income; yet I couldn't shake the thought that theirs was a financial problem. The figure fifty was before me!

"Okay, Lord," I prayed out loud. "If You want me to, I'll give fifty dollars to Danny tomorrow."

I arrived home at 11:45, and Ona served milk and cookies at the kitchen table. I told her about the strong urge to give fifty dollars to Danny and Judi.

"In fact," I said, putting the half-empty glass of milk on the table, "I'm sure I'm supposed to call Danny right now and tell him." I looked at the clock on the wall. 11:55. I shook my head. "It's too late to call; I'll do it tomorrow." I looked at Ona and felt a bit silly. "Funny thing," I said. "God seems to be telling me to call them now."

Ona smiled. "What are you waiting for?" she asked. "The Lord is no respecter of hours!"

Another God Squad couple had a housing problem too. There was the question of where Frank and Marsha would live after they were married. Marsha had her own opinion.

"I'm praying about the girls' house," she told me. "You'll need a couple to live there."

We had made a bid on the mansion in Germantown, and the woman who owned the house had accepted our offer. The only hitch was the zoning board, and they seemed to be taking forever to make up their mind.

Then one night Karen, Kathy, and Marsha were praying in the chapel about a solution to the deadlock with the zoning board. Suddenly Karen stood up.

"Girls!" she cried, "Don't you know that God can provide

a miracle if we just believe? We need to claim the property for Him—remember Jericho!"

Eagerly they leafed through their Bibles. There it was, in Joshua, chapter six, the story of how the Israelites marched around Jericho seven times claiming it for the Lord—and the walls came tumbling down.

"Let's go," Karen cried. "Let's go claim it right now."

It was after midnight, and the rain was pouring down. The three girls climbed into a car and drove to Germantown. There was the house, dark and silent behind the high stone wall. The girls looked up and down the deserted street. There were still lights in the windows next door. What would the neighbors think if they happened to look out?

Kathy giggled. "The neighbors will think we've gone out of our minds."

"Let them," Marsha declared. "We're just doing what God tells us to do, claim the promised land, house, furniture and all, for Him. He'll take care of the rest."

Karen marched ahead; the others followed, and as they marched they began to sing:

> "We are able to go out and take the property,
> to possess the land, the furniture, and house.
> Though giants may be there to hinder,
> He'll surely bring the victory."

Seven times they marched; then soaking wet, but over-joyed, they drove back to the center.

"I just can't wait," Marsha said, "to see how God works it out."

During the next week the girls went back up to Germantown several times, marching around the house and singing their theme song. The neighbors were looking, but the girls came back believing God had already promised, that it would just be a matter of days now.

One day the realtor called.

"Congratulations," he said. "The zoning board has just given you permission to buy the house in Germantown. You are most fortunate. The decision is really quite unexpected."

I smiled as I hung up the phone. Unexpected? I would like to see the zoning board that tried to go against God—

We went up to inspect the property once more—now that we knew it was ours. Ona took my hand as we walked through the spacious rooms with the high ceilings and the view out over flowering bushes, lawns, and trees.

"Do you remember the mansion we picked several years ago?" she asked.

I nodded. How well I remembered! I'd felt so certain then, so cocksure of myself as I laid my plans for the future.

Ona smiled. "It wasn't nearly as nice as this one, was it? Aren't you glad God slammed the door?"

I rubbed my nose and laughed.

No, I wouldn't forget so easily. *How typical of God to do it this way,* I thought.

When I ran ahead of Him, there was the slammed door, the wrong timing.

This time we had asked that God find a house—and He'd led us right back to the same neighborhood, the same zoning laws, the same zoning board, only this time—

"I get your point, Lord." I said it out loud and squeezed

Ona's hand. "I'll wait on You and be of good cheer. You'll give us everything we need."

The next week the lesson became even clearer. I had called the staff together and discussed how we could manage to get a loan for another van. It would be necessary to have transportation for the girls' house, and I was getting concerned about our finances—again.

"Have you prayed about it yet?" Sunday looked at me over the stack of bills, and I coughed slightly while Ona fought to hide a smile.

"Let's pray now," I said, and we all joined hands.

"Thank you, God, for the house," I prayed. "I'm sorry I worried about transportation. Thank You for the way You're going to take care of that hurdle."

The phone rang at my elbow. The polite voice at the other end said, "This is Finch. A few months ago God impressed me to order a van for your center. It's on the car lot now, and I wonder if you would like to pick it up."

I had never met Mr. Finch. He lived in a town in New Jersey and had read about our center in the newspaper.

"We'll pick it up," I said into the phone. "Praise the Lord, and may God bless you."

The van was custom-made. We would never have thought of buying an expensive model like that. Yet it was perfect for our girls, easy to maneuver, riding smoothly as a car.

God says, "Don't worry over anything you need, just tell Me. I'll take care of it."

He means business. We know.

EPILOGUE

GOD isn't finished with His job in Philadelphia, and He isn't through with the God Squad.

Some of the God Squad members have gone on to serve God elsewhere, and new workers have come to join us.

God calls us, He prepares us, and He never leaves us dangling.

Our world is a battlefield where the forces of good are fighting the forces of evil, the light fighting the dark, the real fighting the phony.

God has called every one of us to come alive in Him, to become the light of this world, to expose the counterfeit. In Philadelphia we are dealing specifically with the world of addiction to drugs, alcohol, sex, and boredom!

The battle goes on around the world—in your school, in your community too. And God does call you.

Are you willing? He will make you able.

Every city needs to hear the cry, "Here comes the God Squad!"

*   *   *

If you wish to share in the work of THE GOD SQUAD or need counseling write to:

Bob Bartlett
Teen Challenge
1620 Broad Street
Philadelphia, Pa. 19121